Words of Praise fc
Every Move You Ma

D1479763

"Nikki Winston has developed a lasting method for improving relationships by simply changing the way we move. I've worked with Nikki for years doing the movements and changing my life. When things aren't going right in my life, I know that doing certain movements will help put my life back in balance."
— **Sally Jessy Raphaël,** TV talk-show host

"Nikki Winston is a wondrous star! Through her, I learned to face my fears and found my life open to wider horizons. Her movements to music and her affirmations start my day and fill me with the joyful feeling of balance and harmony. You'll love her inspiration and wisdom!"
— **Ardie Rodale,** chairman, Rodale Inc.; columnist, *Prevention* magazine

*"**Every Move You Make** is a direct route to a more productive and satisfying life. Psychologists take note: This book could hurt your business!"*
— **Caryn Stark,** psychologist and television personality

"When the Golden Door asked me to produce a video of Nikki Winston and her amazing movements, I didn't know I would also be producing a happier me, by doing the movements along with her. This book will help thousands of others to change their lives for the better."
— **Marie Kelly,** producer/director, Kelly Productions International

*"**Every Move You Make** is a much-needed book in such stressful times. Nikki shows us how to move body, mind, and soul together to create a grace-filled and peaceful life. Beautiful!"*
— **Susan Jeffers, Ph.D.,** author of
Feel the Fear and Do It Anyway and *Embracing Uncertainty*

Every Move You Make

Also by Nikki Winston

The Golden Door's Response to Stress (video), A&G Productions, 1989

. . . ˙ ˙ . . .

Hay House Titles of Related Interest

BOOKS

BODYCHANGE™ : *The 21-Day Fitness Program for Changing Your Body . . .
and Changing Your Life!,* by Montel Williams and Wini Linguvic

FLEX ABILITY: *A Story of Strength and Survival,* by Flex Wheeler, with Cindy Pearlman

HELP ME TO HEAL: *A Practical Guidebook for Patients, Visitors, and Caretakers,*
by Bernie Siegel, M.D., and Yosaif August

SHAPE MAGAZINE'S SHAPE YOUR LIFE, by Barbara Harris,
Editor-in-Chief, *Shape*® magazine, with Angela Hynes

THE TRUTH: *The Only Fitness Book You'll Ever Need,*
by Frank Sepe

ULTIMATE PILATES: *Achieve the Perfect Body Shape,* by Dreas Reyneke

YOGA PURE AND SIMPLE:
Transform Your Body Shape with the Program That Really Works, by Kisen

CARD DECKS/BOXED SETS

8 MINUTES IN THE MORNING® KIT: *A Simple Way to Shed Up to
2 Pounds a Week Guaranteed* (A CD and Card Deck System), by Jorge Cruise

8 MINUTES IN THE MORNING® FOR MAXIMUM WEIGHT LOSS KIT:
A Simple Way for Fuller Figures to Shed Up to 2 Pounds a Week–Guaranteed!
(A CD and Card Deck System), by Jorge Cruise

HEALTHY BODY Cards, by Louise L. Hay

YOGA IN A BOX, by Cyndi Lee
(available in Basic, Intermediate, and Couples programs)

All of the above are available at your local bookstore, or may be ordered by visiting:
Hay House USA: **www.hayhouse.com;** Hay House Australia: **www.hayhouse.com.au;**
Hay House UK: **www.hayhouse.co.uk**; or Hay House South Africa: **orders@psdprom.co.za**

Every Move You Make

Bodymind Exercises to Transform Your Life

Nikki Winston

HAY HOUSE, INC.
Carlsbad, California
London • Sydney • Johannesburg
Vancouver • Hong Kong

Published and distributed in the United States by: Hay House, Inc., P.O. Box 5100, Carlsbad, CA 92018-5100 • *Phone:* (760) 431-7695 or (800) 654-5126 • *Fax:* (760) 431-6948 or (800) 650-5115 • www.hayhouse.com • **Published and distributed in Australia by:** Hay House Australia Ltd., 18/36 Ralph St., Alexandria NSW 2015 • *Phone:* 612-9669-4299 • *Fax:* 612-9669-4144 • www.hayhouse.com.au • **Published and distributed in the United Kingdom by:** Hay House UK, Ltd. • Unit 202, Canalot Studios • 222 Kensal Rd., London W10 5BN • *Phone:* 44-20-8962-1230 • *Fax:* 44-20-8962-1239 • www.hayhouse.co.uk • **Published and distributed in the Republic of South Africa by:** Hay House SA (Pty), Ltd., P.O. Box 990, Witkoppen 2068 • *Phone/Fax:* 2711-7012233 • orders@psdprom.co.za • **Distributed in Canada by:** Raincoast • 9050 Shaughnessy St., Vancouver, B.C. V6P 6E5 • *Phone:* (604) 323-7100 • *Fax:* (604) 323-2600

Editorial supervision: Jill Kramer
Design: Summer McStravick
Photography: Gregory Bertolini

Library of Congress Cataloging-in-Publication Data

Winston, Nikki
  Every move you make : body, mind exercises to transform your life / Nikki Winston.
    p. cm.
  ISBN 1-4019-0119-0 (trade paper)
  1. Exercise. 2. Mind and body. I. Title.
  GV481.W59 2003
  613.7'1—dc21
                          2002155127

                    ISBN 1-4019-0119-0

            06 05 04 03   4 3 2 1
              1st printing, October 2003

          Printed in the United States of America

To Michael—my love, laugh, and dance partner

Contents

Editor's Note: To avoid the awkward he/she construction,
the feminine pronoun has been used predominantly throughout this book.

Part I

Change the Way You Move...
and Change Your Life

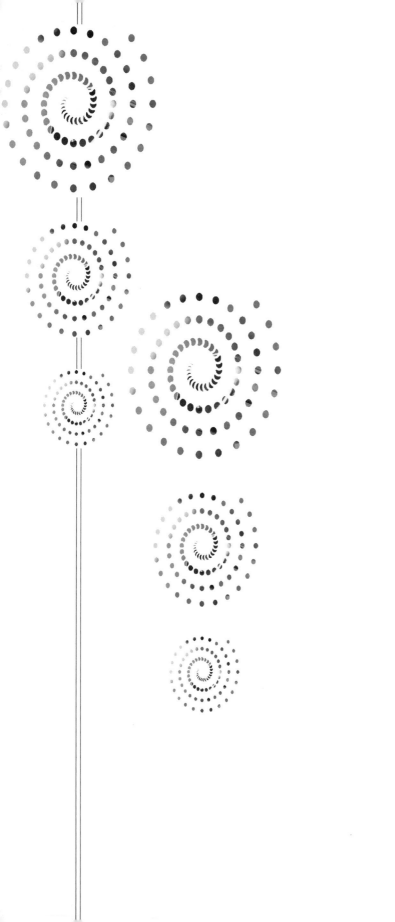

Chapter One

Come Home
to a New You

"We shall not cease from exploration

And the end of all our exploring

Will be to arrive where we started

And know the place for the first time."

— from "Little Gidding" by T. S. Eliot

Is your life the way you want it to be? Are you the person you want to be, the person you're certain you can be, the person you know you really are inside? Since you're reading a book about how to transform yourself and your life, I'm going to guess that the answer is no.

Something is "off-center" for you. Maybe it's your job, your relationship, or your *lack* of a relationship. Perhaps your days are filled with the "shoulds" and "should nots" of obligation, leaving no time for the "want tos" of pleasure and desire. Maybe you sense that you're not succeeding in your life or your career as you had hoped to, as you know you could—if only things were different. You feel frustrated, pressured, encumbered, and adrift.

Don't look now, but it shows—in *every move you make*.

I mean that quite literally. The way you stand, sit, walk, and hold yourself all reflect your inner life. It's the bodymind connection—the link between the way you feel and your physical state. Because of that link, your thoughts and emotions program themselves into the way you move your body. You've seen it in others—the drooping shoulders of someone who's dejected, the briskly upright walk of someone who's happy or successful, the careless seated posture of someone with low self-esteem. And you see it in yourself: When you're under stress, the tension goes right to the back of your neck or into your shoulders; when you're worried, your jaw locks; and anger tightens your abdominal muscles until you feel that you can hardly breathe. In fact, the way you move sends all sorts of messages about your feelings and gives all kinds of clues about your sense of self—and you can read your life in every move you make.

This book will help you change the story your movements tell. Its promise is both simple and revolutionary: Change your movement, and you can literally change your life. You can unblock frustration, lighten pressure, free yourself of your encumbrances, find your own anchor—and bring yourself and your life to where you want them to be.

How? In a way, it's as elementary as smiling to make yourself feel better. You don't believe me? Try it. Go ahead—stretch the corners of your mouth upward, part your lips, and mouth the word *cheese*.

You *do* feel better—more cheerful—don't you?

Stand up (if you're not already). Square those shoulders and stretch that neck. Lift your chin and hold your head erect. It's a pretty safe bet that your emotions straightened up with you. You now feel tall, forthright, and in charge.

Now frown. Curl the corners of your mouth downward and bring your lips together stiffly. Let your eyelids drop and your shoulders droop, and stretch your neck muscles taut with vexed discontent.

Guess what—vexed discontent is going to be what you feel.

Small changes of no great significance? Perhaps. But they demonstrate the point that by changing your physical state, you can change your mental or emotional focus as well.

Usually when we seek change in life, we begin with the mental or emotional. We try to analyze what's wrong, and we explore our psyche and feelings to find the source of our dissatisfaction or dysfunction so that we can work to change it. Well, there's nothing wrong with that. It's essentially the same thing I'm suggesting in this book. But this time, we're going to find what's wrong through physical movement, and we're going to change what needs changing by altering the way we move.

For example, Libby was a seriously overweight woman who had spent a lifetime trying and failing to lose weight. As I put her through a sequence of movements, her body spoke volumes to me, but one movement was particularly loud and clear. Whenever Libby tried a movement that suggested "letting go," her fists tightened, and she "held on" as hard as she could. Together, we worked on changing the physical movement. As Libby learned to ease her fists, thereby loosening her grip on the things she was holding, her feelings also began to change . . . and she started losing weight. We began to work on other movements that helped her deal with what she was afraid of losing—what the weight represented in other ways. By shifting patterns programmed into her body long ago, Libby has learned to let go of the excess baggage weighing down her spirit *and* her body.

Moving Affirmations

At the core of this book is a set of ten exercises I call Moving Affirmations. They're specifically aimed at helping you deal with the particular issue that leaves you feeling that you're not living life to the fullest. Of course, at different stages of your life, the issue you want to focus on may shift as circumstances change and as you evolve as a person. Today's issue might be how to handle stress; a year from today, it might be how to inject more passion into your relationship. Whatever the focus of the moment, this book will show you how to use these Moving Affirmations to shift your feelings, release inhibiting patterns, heal dysfunctions, and come home to the person you know you can be. You'll learn to change the way you move *intentionally*—and thus change what's going on in your mind, heart, spirit, and soul. You'll enjoy more peace and greater success, and your life will change for the better.

A client of mine named Robert was one of those high-powered executives for whom it's always "decision time"—with millions of dollars, countless products, and hundreds of people's jobs dependent on every choice. For Robert, the intentional movements we worked on together became a tool for gaining perspective, clearing his mind of clutter, and coming back to the essence of himself—to his own center and to the central issue with which he must deal.

So now, when a meeting becomes too noisy and the pressure too great, Robert excuses himself, heads for the men's room, stands before the mirror, and goes through the simple movement that speaks to him at such moments. He notices right away if, for example, his shoulders remain high and tight as he circles his arms wide before him. "Adjust," he tells himself, and as he does, he feels his shoulders unlock, his brain open up, and his tension settle into peaceful calm as his muscles loosen. After just a few minutes of movement, Robert gains a broader perspective on the business issues of the day and their role in his life. He re-equips himself with fresh vision so that he can make decisions rationally, sensibly, and coolly. The decisions are better—and Robert's *life* is better, too.

There's nothing difficult about these Moving Affirmations. They're not rigorous contortions or high-powered activities that will leave you panting for breath and dripping with sweat. They don't require any special skill, and you don't need the body of a gymnast or the grace of a ballerina to do them. They're simple, gentle, deliberate motions that you can learn easily by following the written instructions and referring to the photographs that illustrate each movement. Mastery will come simply through practicing the movements over and over. The more you do them, the more proficient you'll become. And once you're doing the Moving Affirmations fluidly, deliberately, and joyously, you'll feel a sense of peace, a balance and wholeness, and a *youness* that will add value to each day of your life. I promise.

My Moving Affirmations

How can I make such a promise? For one thing, it happened to me.

Like a lot of the students I work with today, I sought a career in the fast lane. Armed with an MBA degree, I quickly reached a high rung on the corporate ladder and had all the accoutrements of what's generally considered success. I was in my late 20s, vice president of a Madison Avenue advertising agency, financially secure, and a rising star on the cutting edge of my profession. I was also the embodiment of stress—although I didn't realize it. I did know that I was under a lot of pressure, that I was suspicious of my own achievements, that I secretly feared I was in way over my head, and my marriage was in trouble—probably as a result of the pressure and doubt.

A friend suggested that I attend a Tai Ji (frequently written as T'ai Chi) class. At the time, I knew almost nothing about the Chinese practice of Tai Ji. I was aware that it had caught on as a gentle form of exercise accessible to all ages, as it requires no particular skill or athletic prowess. I'd heard that it was relaxing, good for the circulation, limbering, and a nice way to stretch—a good break from the stresses and strains of daily life. I had no idea that Tai Ji was an ancient discipline at the heart of an elaborate system of philosophy. Had I known, I almost certainly wouldn't have taken up my friend's suggestion.

Who needed philosophy and the secrets of the East? All I was looking for was a pleasant evening of relaxing stretches so that I might get rid of some of the stress I felt. Besides, the class was within walking distance of my home, I had nothing else to do that night, and I simply couldn't think of a good reason not to go. So I went, and thus began my own personal voyage of self-knowledge and reconnection with my true essence—a voyage home to myself.

As I learned that night, the odyssey home takes you to your true nature, the part of you that's really you—your physical, emotional, spiritual center. That center is both the starting point and the goal, origin, and destination. You begin life's journey in a state of perfect balance at the center, but the journey itself—with all its frustrations, pressures, and burdens—tilts you off-center, knocking your natural balance askew. It's like a table that stands lopsided because it's been painted and stained and "fixed" so many times that even its legs are uneven; the layers of stain and paint have to be stripped away and scraped out of every corner and crevice before the original, authentic table stands squarely and easily on its own legs. Well, you need to strip away all the layers of restrictions, fears, and regulations that life has painted over you to get back to your authentic self and find your balance at the center. For your center is where your strength is; from there, you're strong enough to do anything. Center yourself physically, and you'll center yourself spiritually and emotionally.

That's what I learned to do in my voyage of self-knowledge—I learned to find harmony with the world within me and the environment all around me. Such harmony brings with it a sense of calm, strength, and safety. It empowers me to deal with whatever life has in store for me. And it feels absolutely wonderful.

Yet the journey continues. The advertising job is long gone, the marriage is more happily secure than ever, and what began in that first Tai Ji class has been augmented, modified, and refashioned into my own innovative form of movement practice. It has been my joy over the decades since that first class to share this technique with people of all ages, professions, and backgrounds. Through practice, my students have been able to resolve particular issues or problems, reduce stress, ease or eliminate physical and mental pain, increase their energy and vitality, and reconnect with nature's healing forces. They've gained clarity about what they want, and they enjoy happier, healthier, and more fulfilling lives through the work we do together—work they continue on their own. They've found, as I have, the true success of coming home to themselves.

You will, too.

Tony was a guy who almost literally had the ground pulled out from under him. As a young man, he'd climbed onto the roof of a building under construction one summer morning. Exploring among the stacks of lumber and sacks of concrete, he'd stepped back, lost his footing, and had fallen several stories to the ground. He barely escaped death. Tony was unconscious for days and out of commission for several weeks. And for the rest of his life thereafter, he lived in a state of anxiety, haunted by a deep-rooted feeling that the ground under his feet was about to give way. In his subconscious mind, nothing was stable, nothing could last, and everything was threatened.

The feeling became its own self-fulfilling prophecy: Tony's business ventures, love relationships, and even his dealings with friends were regularly disrupted and often failed. The anxiety stored in his body from this early trauma affected the very manner in which he lived—and it was reflected in the way he moved.

I saw this uneasiness in one of the movements I asked Tony to do the very first time he came to my studio. It was a movement aimed at helping people open their hearts and minds to receive and embrace new possibilities. "Step back," I instructed, but Tony stood still. "Just set one foot behind the other," I offered. Yet again, Tony couldn't move. I tried a third time: "Take this foot and place it here." Still, Tony was rooted in place. "Is everything okay?" I finally asked.

"Fine," he answered genially.

"Did anything ever happen to you that had to do with stepping backward?"

Tony shook his head. "No. Nothing."

"Let's try it again," I suggested. "Very simply, very gently . . . just step back." With great concentration, Tony did so, and as he did, his expression grew calm.

"There was something once," he blurted out, and he told me the story of his early accident. That was the breakthrough we needed—the understanding that what affects the body affects the mind affects the body and back again. With that, we began changing the way Tony moved and started changing his life. In time, a new mobility broke the choke hold that anxiety had put around Tony's being—and transformed every aspect of his life for the better.

Your Moving Affirmations—and More

As your life evolves, the issues with which you must deal shift. The fact is that at some point in your life, you'll face every one of them. Today it might be career, stress, or a control issue; tomorrow it might be fears or anxieties, hitting a dead end in your work life, or a giant wall in your creative life. One way or another, at one time or another, every chapter in this book will speak to you, so focus on the chapter or chapters that address whatever issue is in the forefront of your life.

Here's what you'll find in each of the chapters:

- **A narrative** about the aspect of experience that the movement addresses.

- **Case studies** of real-life students I've worked with who have had a problem with this aspect of experience. (Their names have been changed and the details of their lives altered to protect their privacy.)

- Suggestions for the **Moving Affirmations** that will help you deal with issues, work through problems, and give wings to your potential. These Moving Affirmations are aimed at releasing the blockages and peeling away the layers of conditioned restraints on your movement and flexibility in body and mind. They'll bring you closer to the true core of who you are, so that with changed perspective, you can reconnect to the joy that's hidden within you. To do the affirmations, follow these three steps (a good way to remember the order of these actions is that their first letters spell out the message "I AM"):

  1. **Intend** a positive desired outcome to energize your sense of purpose. So rather than the negative "I don't want to feel constrained," say "I intend to feel free."

  2. **Affirm** the change you're seeking through a word or phrase that resonates for you. For example, you might affirm that "I can create the life I want." You'll see more such affirmations addressing common issues in Appendix A. Find one that speaks to your situation or make up your own.

  3. **Move** in the particular sequence of motions that addresses the change you seek.

In addition, I'll often suggest an image that you can picture to help you feel the movement on a deeper level, and thus prepare the ground to support your transformation.

Although it's not required, I often play music as I practice the moving affirmations. In Appendix B, you'll find a list of some of my favorite music, which is all readily available.

Over time, as you do the Moving Affirmations called for in the chapter and you gain smoothness with repetition and mastery with concentration, you'll remodel your body. And soon enough, you'll feel the change in your mind and your emotions. Later you may want to practice the Moving Affirmations from beginning to end without stopping after each segment. To help you with this practice, I've included the entire series, uninterrupted, in Appendix C.

In addition to the Moving Affirmations for transforming your life, this book offers a number of movements devoted specifically to relationships and sex. For these you'll need a partner. While it may be theoretically possible to *imagine* your partner, imagination is nothing like the reality of being in a relationship with someone.

Finally, this book will also teach you some additional movements to help you let go and flow with life. It offers guidance as you begin to program the concept of movement practice into your life, establishing a solid context for the changes that will continue to happen.

Alone or with a partner, using Moving Affirmations or partner movement, you'll repattern your body, mind, emotions, and spirit. Not just so you can work better, but so you can live better; not just to help "fix" a problem, but also to stave off the complications of the spirit that seem to plague our era; not just to improve your life around the edges, but to actually change your life so that you're living the life you've always wanted.

Will it work? You bet it will. I've seen it succeed time and time again—in my own life, and in the lives of corporate executives, resort vacationers, celebrities, and the hundreds of students I work with in my practice.

Want to know exactly *how* it works? Read on.

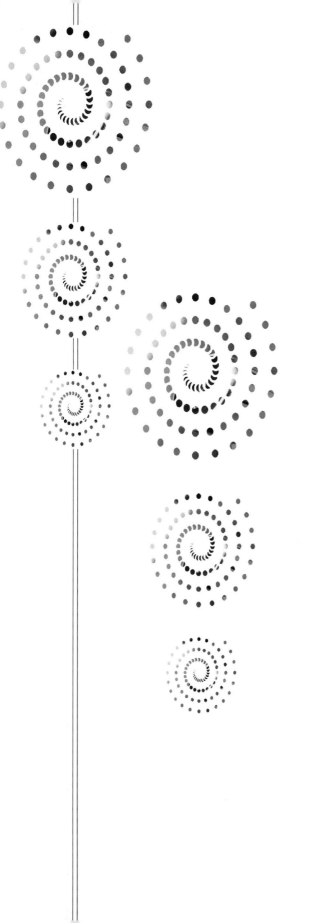

Chapter Two

How Changing Your Movements Will Change Your Life

"They always say only time changes things,

but you actually have to change them yourself."

— Andy Warhol

Want to understand why and how changing your movements will change your life? Then this chapter is for you. If, on the other hand, you'd rather get right into the details of the movements, or you're eager to move on to the chapter focusing on the specific issue in the forefront of your life right now, feel free to skip ahead. Either way works; this book has been designed to allow you to follow your personal inclinations.

You already know half of the explanation of how your life relates to your movements: Tension tightens the muscles and limits flexibility, while confidence loosens the body and lets you move with fluid ease—emotional distress and emotional well-being show up in the way you move. Chances are that you're perfectly prepared to believe that by changing your mental concentration and/or emotional circumstances, you can actually alter your physical condition. After all, turn on ESPN almost any time of the day and you'll hear a star athlete claiming that mental focus is the key to physical performance, or a coach talking about getting his team "psyched" for an upcoming game.

Perhaps you've even heard about the medical therapy advanced by the late Norman Cousins. In the 1960s, Cousins found himself diagnosed with a severe connective-tissue disease. He rejected his doctors' treatments, and instead fed himself a steady diet of *Candid Camera* reruns and Marx Brothers movies. As a result, he claimed that "ten minutes of genuine belly laughter had an anesthetic effect and would give me at least two hours of pain-free sleep." He recovered from the disease and went on to continue his research on the mind-body connection as adjunct professor of Medical Humanities at the UCLA School of Medicine.

In the late 1970s and early '80s, Dr. John Sarno, professor of Clinical Rehabilitation Medicine at the New York University School of Medicine, caused something of a sensation with his radical—and effective—approach to diagnosing and healing back pain. Based on the neurophysiology of mind-body disorder, Sarno contended that emotions such as guilt, anxiety, depression, and low self-esteem caused the brain to manufacture such physical symptoms as migraine headaches, muscle pain, repetitive strain injuries, even hay fever. Needless to say, Sarno's recovery plan for patients doesn't rely on medication, but rather on "exposing the undercover operation"—the emotional cause of the disorder—"and thereby ending it." (You'll be doing something very similar when you practice the Moving Affirmations that make up my movement practice.)

Sarno's groundbreaking work and all the laboratory studies that followed it made the mind-body approach an accepted part of medical practice and teaching. In fact, from Maine to California, our finest universities and medical schools now teach the power of mind and feeling over the body, and the power of changing mind and feeling to affect the body.

It's strange, then, to think that our culture doesn't readily accept the other half of the mind-body connection—the idea that physical action can affect our mental and emotional state so that changing the way we move changes the way we think and feel. We haven't yet embraced the rather obvious lesson that the bodymind connection is a *reciprocal link*. It goes both ways, a fact that's worth repeating: Change your mental or emotional focus, and you can change your physical state; by the same token, *change your physical state, and you can change your mental or emotional focus.*

Movement As Message

Watch a baby move—it's the most natural thing in the world. Squirming, stretching, reaching, turning, rolling—a baby's movements are nature in motion. What you're watching is someone utterly at home in his or her own skin, and completely connected to his or her surroundings. Every shift, every stirring, every bit of bustle is entirely aligned with the baby's nature, which is totally spontaneous, and still unconditioned by any external influences apart from the natural needs of survival—eating, sleeping, and cuddling.

From a very early age, however, the conditioning input begins: restrictions, prohibitions, qualifications, and limits. Sit still. Walk, don't run. Stop squirming. Don't touch. No hopping. No skipping. No ball-playing in the house. Don't sit with your legs crossed. Be careful, don't wrinkle your dress! Stand up straight. Get down from there. Keep out of the woods. Stay between the lines. Don't scuff those new shoes. Go to your room! Each instruction takes you just a little bit further away from your true nature, from the natural movement that governed you as a baby and from your sense of connection to the world around you. This conditioning input gets coded into your internal makeup as blockages to what's most natural in you; and over the years, the blockages build up, layer upon layer.

Yet it isn't just instructions from your elders that condition you away from natural movement—it's your entire life experience. The losses, the rejections, and the disappointments you suffer all plant themselves in the body, and eventually bear fruit as movement. So do your triumphs and glories. Everything that has to do with your sense of yourself mentally and emotionally shows up in the way you bear yourself physically. You've heard the term "muscle memory"? Who you are isn't just in your brain, but in your muscles, too—in fact, it's in every bit of your cells, sinews, tissue, skin, and bones.

But you don't have to take my word for it. All of this—the entire bodymind issue—is the focus of intense medical research into the information pathways in the body, the ways in which intellectual, physical, and emotional data circulates, and how organs and systems affect each other as a result. One of the most prominent of the researchers on this subject is Dr. Candace B. Pert, Georgetown University Medical Center research professor and former chief of the Section on Brain Biochemistry at the National Institutes of

Health. Pert argues that the receptors first identified in the neurons of the brain, the so-called neuropeptide receptors, are actually found in the tissues of all the other systems of the body as well—including the immune system, the hormonal system, and the digestive system.

In effect, Pert's research shows that many of the functions traditionally attributed to the brain actually originate elsewhere in the body, and these receptor molecules travel throughout the body, carrying messages from system to system. The receptors, Pert says, are really the physical or physiological parallels of feelings of stress, anger, hunger, energy, depression, happiness—you name it. In fact, in Pert's view, we shouldn't be speaking of any separation at all between the physiological and the emotional, between body and mind. Pert calls her book on the subject *Molecules of Emotion,*[1] which is her name for those receptors charging around our bodies, carrying messages of physical health or illness and emotional well-being or gloom. And since the physical and the emotional can't be separated, Pert calls the whole the "bodymind"—a perfect description, I think, for the idea that the body-mind connection is a reciprocal, bidirectional link that operates as an ongoing loop.

At the Golden Door

Molecules of Emotion was ten years away from publication when I began teaching my movement practice at the world-famous Golden Door spa near San Diego. Each week I'd meet a fresh new class of 25 or so people—mostly women—who were eager to gain the health benefits of Tai Ji's gentle movement. After a while, I noticed that certain movement patterns recurred with an almost punctual regularity in group after group, week after week.

Of course, it isn't particularly surprising that similarities cropped up. The women who come to the Golden Door share some fundamental demographics. They tend to be high-powered individuals leading lives of great visibility and achievement. Many of them hold important positions in major organizations, many are successful entrepreneurs, and many are celebrities who live in the public eye. Many are also overweight, stressed, and anxious, with unsuccessful or even self-destructive relationships, low self-esteem, and feelings of worthlessness.

The recurring patterns of movement reflected these issues and pointed to their source. One woman in particular seemed to typify the phenomenon—I'll call her Joan. In the movement called Sky and Earth, in which we reach out to the natural world beyond and the solid earth beneath, then bring both to our center, Joan could reach out above and below, but couldn't bring sky and earth back to the center. She kept "giving" it all away. Where the movement called for bringing the hands toward a point just below the navel, Joan instead pushed her hands outward, away from her body.

In fact, in every movement reflecting *any* kind of self-nurturing, Joan's body simply wouldn't—or couldn't—bring vital nourishment home to herself.

The message was clear, one that's been programmed into the code of many women: *Take care of everyone else first—husband, children, parents, neighbors, job, volunteer assignment—before you take care of yourself.* Get the kids to soccer, karate, ballet, and band practice before you get yourself to the gym or a massage. Attend to your husband's needs—his comfort, physical fitness, and sense of self-worth—before you take care of your own. As noble as this sounds, it's a sure path to throwing your life off balance.

That was exactly the case with many women at the Golden Door—and certainly with Joan. When I began to talk to her about it, she suddenly became very articulate about her lack of inner nourishment. It all poured out of her: For some time, she'd felt sapped of energy, strength, and vitality. Then, just before she came to the spa, she'd been given dreadful news: a diagnosis of breast cancer. Having seen in her movements how startlingly out-of-balance she was, my guess was that the cancer diagnosis had put an already susceptible woman over the edge.

Right then and there, Joan and I began to work on changing her movements. The cancer diagnosis had galvanized Joan's focus, and she was now intensely motivated to make a change. She worked hard—almost fiercely—with great concentration and conscientiousness. By the time she left the spa, at least she was no longer running on empty; the adjusted movements had siphoned a bit of fuel back into the tank. Joan and I continued to work together one-on-one at my studio, and as the weeks went by, she began to feel better. Her medical reports also improved, and after some months, Joan's cancer went into remission. More than 15 years later, she remains cancer free, healthy, and emotionally and spiritually balanced.

To me, this was a powerfully dramatic manifestation of the connection between emotion and illness, and of the reciprocal link Candace Pert called "bodymind." A decade after I taught my first class at the Golden Door, I heard Pert explaining her research on a Bill Moyers show about healing and the mind, and it rang a bell that powerfully reminded me of Joan. Pert asserted that the body is actually the unconscious mind. Therefore, when a repressed trauma caused by an overwhelming emotion stores itself in the body and becomes locked inside, the consequences are felt in both body and mind—in bodymind.

This seemed to me to be exactly what had happened to Joan, and what happens to so many others to lesser or greater extent: She could feel neither the part of the body that was "sick" nor the emotional correlation, because her emotions had snapped shut a door and closed all the energy inside. Only by shifting her movements could Joan release the energy—the life force that brings health to the mind, body, and spirit.

Pert's work articulated in scientific terms what I'd seen in action in the bodies and in the lives of student after student. It confirmed medically what my students were experiencing physically, emotionally, and spiritually: The mind-body connection is also a body-mind connection. It's not a two-way street, but a loop—a path of motion that keeps circling back on itself.

Awareness + Intention = Transformation

Pert's analysis of the ongoing bodymind loop leads to two important conclusions. First, since the body's movements mirror what's going on in the mind, heart, spirit, and soul, careful observation of the body's movements can teach us a lot about what's going on inside us. We can see where our movements are blocked and can use this awareness to identify the problems, issues, dilemmas, questions, confusions, and hang-ups that plague us or burden our lives. Second, based on that understanding, we can intentionally move the body in different ways. In doing so, we clear the blockages, peel away the layers of conditioned restraints on movement and flexibility, and get closer to our natural selves—to the true center of who we are—and to our connectedness with the natural world. And what happens when we get back to our true nature? We find that we're well prepared to deal with the problems, issues, dilemmas, and so forth. We're ready to rise to any challenge life may throw our way, and we're prepared to connect with the wider world and enter into meaningful and lasting relationships with others.

The Wisdom of the East

The very idea that there might be a barrier between body and mind is a fairly recent invention, and it's found only in Western thinking. It derives from the theory of dualism devised by 17th- and 18th-century European rationalist philosophers, a theory that claims a separation between the spiritual and the material, the mind and the body. It's a separation, as we've seen, that science and medicine are now questioning, and replacing with theories about the interconnectedness of all things, including the systems of the body.

Eastern philosophy never accepted the concept of separating the material and spiritual realms. The sense of the universe as united—even in opposition—is basic to the cultures of the East. The classical Chinese version of this perception speaks of yin and yang, representing all the opposing principles in the universe, in both material and spiritual states: night and day, life and death, north and south, positive and negative electrical charges. Yin principles are receptive, female principles—such as the moon, cold, darkness, submission, and the earth. Yang principles are assertive, male principles—such as the sun, creation, heat, light, and heaven. Each of these opposites produces the other and *requires* the other: Creation occurs under the principle of yang, but the completion of the created thing occurs under yin, and vice versa. Yin produces yang, and yang produces yin, and the producing occurs cyclically and constantly. No one principle dominates all the time; no one principle determines the other all the time. Everything you experience—health and sickness, wealth and poverty, power and submission—can be explained as just the temporary dominance of one principle over the other, and everything you experience is subject to change into its opposite.

In short, it's a loop. Yin and yang act, react, and counteract. Action leads to reaction, and when the reaction ends, the direction is changed, and the loop of action, reaction, and counteraction begins again—or rather, it continues. Opposites must be in balance, like magnets going head to head. In people, mind and body are one and should be in equal balance.

Elaborate systems of physical activity based in these principles have been developed over thousands of years in Asia. Tai Ji was developed in China toward the end of the Sung Dynasty (929-1297) as a martial art combining techniques of self-protection—originally against potential attacks from beasts of the forest—and guidance for living a healthy life. Qigong (pronounced *chee-gong*) is another Chinese practice—one depicted in rock paintings that date back 4,000 years. It focuses on cultivating energy—the energy that circulates in us and between our body and our surroundings. That vital energy is fully present in babies, but life's stresses and strains sap it as we grow up and grow older. The fluid movements, breathing exercises, and visualizations that comprise Qigong technique are aimed at releasing these blockages and renewing the vital energy of life.

Shintaido, "the new body way," is a much newer practice. Developed in Japan in the 1960s by a group that included martial artists, musicians, actors, and others, Shintaido is a system of physical culture that embraces healing, creativity and human potential, martial arts, and the pursuit of world peace and mutual understanding. It's all grounded in body movement—a way to find one's true self, to communicate with others, and to become unified with nature.

Tai Ji, Qigong, and Shintaido are the basis of my movement practice. The reason is simple: These movements reconnect us to our center—the naturally integrated bodymind and vital energy with which we're born—and to the basic elements of the wider world.

To create my movement practice, I've refined and recast the core of these disciplines, added some movements from other practices, and incorporated much of what I've learned through my experience with hundreds upon hundreds of students. And I've crystallized it all into the ten Moving Affirmations, the partnered work, and the additional movements that will enhance your ability to make change.

Going Home

In Chapter 1, I asked you to smile in order to feel its cheering effects. Do it again—it works, lifting your spirits. This intentional movement, out of all the millions of unconscious movements a day, has affected your perception and changed your feelings.

As you read this book, you'll learn about intentional movements that will let you step back and look inside yourself, open up to look around you, reach out for what you need from the universe, bring its essence into your own, and let your inner light expand and shine. You'll be introduced to intentional movements that let you soar, freed from every-day concerns so that you can see the world from the eagle's vantage, then return to earth, embrace what life has to offer, and come home to your own mountaintop—solid, grounded, with a spectacular view. You'll think about intentional movements in every move you make to clear the mind, replace stress with calmness, heal the spirit, and unleash and ignite your true potential—so that every step you take will bring you closer to the possibility of transforming your precious life for the better.

Are you ready? Let's begin.

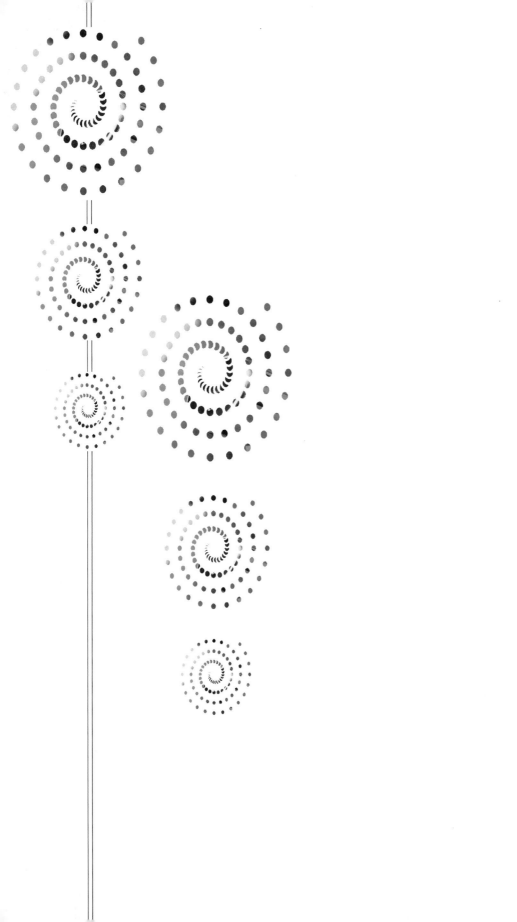

Chapter Three

Getting Centered

"Every time you don't follow your

inner guidance, you feel a loss of energy,

loss of power, a sense of spiritual deadness."

— Shakti Gawain

If I were to ask you, "What's the strongest part of the body?" your first, off-the-top-of-your-head answer might be, "The upper body." When you think physical power, you probably conjure up images of broad shoulders, muscled arms, and defined upper chests.

Well, think again. The real source of strength in the body is found in the muscles attached to the pelvic girdle. Ask a javelin thrower or a shot-putter or a Saturday-night bowler—they know that the foundation of their power is the area just below the waist. A runner springs forward from that same center, and rowers work from there as well—when they don't, their rowing arms quickly tire. So, the source of your strength isn't found in your limbs or your extremities, but at the physical center of your body.

When you're truly balanced and your energy emanates from your center, extraordinary things happen. Moving from the physical center of the body is what athletes call being "in the zone," and you may have experienced it yourself. Maybe you were out for a run, playing softball on the Fourth of July, or having a great day on the golf course when suddenly you realized that your body was flowing. You felt absolutely connected to everything around you and moved with ease; there was no struggle. Simply put, you were centered. And the upshot was that you felt you could run forever, the softball seemed like an enormous globe that you could hit every time and field with no effort, or every shot you made from the tee off to the final putt went exactly where you intended.

The center is a place we want to be able to get to more often than once in our lives; in fact, we want to be able to consciously dwell there. To see what being centered feels like, try this with a partner: Stand facing each other, then ask him or her to apply pressure to a point on your shoulder or even at the center of your chest. A light nudge with an open hand is sufficient, there's no need to shove. Even if you're ready and waiting for the sudden pressure, chances are you'll be pushed off the spot where you're standing. If that happens, it means that you were off center and out of balance, because when you're off center, you're easily toppled.

Try the exercise again, but this time place your hands just below your navel and focus your mind on that spot in your body. Relax your breathing and your muscles, and drop your arms to your sides. Keep your mind on your center and your body relaxed. Now ask your partner to try to nudge you again. This time, he or she will find you immovable, unshakable, and unassailable. Focusing on the center has put you in balance, and it's more difficult to topple something or someone that's in balance.

Living from the Center

Most people assume that their center is located in the brain or the heart. That would make them pretty top-heavy. Instead, think about where you come from physically—the womb, which gives life. An umbilical cord connected you to the center of your mother just as an umbilical cord connected her to the center of her mother—and so on, back into your past. *That's* the center of your body, your point of origin, your nexus of connection.

Finding your center doesn't mean giving up your brain or heart, though. On the contrary. It provides a base of support—like a "third leg"—that keeps brain and heart in balance. I like the description offered by George Leonard, a fifth-degree black belt in aikido, in his book, *The Way of Aikido*[2]: "To be centered is to say yes to life. The center joins past and future, heaven and earth, the near and the far, the way out and the way in. It is a secure place from which to venture forth and to which you can always return."

So it's not surprising that getting in touch with your center makes you feel safe. Until you feel safe, you really can't make a move in life; you're paralyzed. That's why it's important to focus on your center when you do the Moving Affirmations—it will help you enhance the fluidity of your movements and bolster your energy.

One of my clients, Philip, was a current-events junkie who went ballistic over the news. Watching television newscasts wound him as tight as a violin string, and reading the morning paper clenched his entire body. The effect was so total that he thought the only answer might be to turn off the television and cancel his newspaper subscription. But I had another suggestion: He should keep on learning what was happening in the world, but not become so caught up in it.

In our very first session, I had Philip practice focusing on his center—nothing else. When Philip went home that day, he noticed an immediate change: The nightly news didn't send him around the bend. In the next session, we continued the focus on his center but also practiced the Wood movement, which is all about bending with the world but not being broken by it (instructions for this movement are found in Part II). I asked Philip to let his body open and his arms and eyes expand outward while he kept his attention on his center. Within weeks, Philip had gained a core of security. He was still a news junkie, but instead of being paralyzed by world events, he was able to go out and meet the issues rationally.

When you feel safe and energized, your confidence will soar. Think about the people you've met or known whose entrance into a room seemed to charge the air with currents of light and heat. Inevitably, these are people with a strong sense of self, people so connected to their own center that they can move out from there easily, happily, eager to deal with whatever they confront, and confident that they can always find their way back to center again. Getting centered is a path to such confidence. You'll see the world with greater clarity, find that life feels less demanding, and stop "sweating the small stuff," because you know you can handle it. It is indeed small stuff.

Finding Your Center

Tai Ji defines your center as running through three points of your body. First and foremost is your actual physical center at a point just below your navel. The Chinese word for this center—and the word I'll use throughout the book—is *tantien* (pronounced *don-tyen*). The second point up is level with your heart and in the middle of your chest—it's the heartmind center. The third anchoring point is the so-called third eye, your spiritual center. It's located in the middle of your forehead, just above your eyebrows.

Now picture a column of light running through all three points, perfectly aligned, and holding all the centers in balance. That's where you want to be—on that axis running straight up from the tantien, through the heartmind, through the third eye, and continuing onward up to the sky and all the way down into the earth. When all three centers are connected and the anchoring points are linked, you're truly centered and you feel safe. The world around you goes on, but how you relate to it is different—its issues and events can't topple you because you're centered.

Find your tantien center now. Start an inch or so below your navel, and focus. Go inside, traveling there in your mind. You're at the source of your spiritual and emotional strength, at the place where the very essence of your self resides. Hold the spot in your mind's eye and send a message to your center from your mind: Your body is ready to be in balance and harmony. Feel your center and concentrate. It's unique, your special place, the core of you. So find it and enjoy it.

Centering Exercises

Now try this variation on a Tai Ji movement called the Golden Lotus. It's a great way to center yourself, and I recommend taking the time for it once a day—maybe as a way to start your morning. Stand relaxed, with your arms down in front of your body, fingers pointing toward the ground, and palms resting lightly on your upper thighs. Move your hands up your body, tracing the line through your centers as you go. As you pass your tantien center, think about the essential *youness* that's there. Then let your hands move up past the heartmind center at your heart level, and on up over your third eye at the center of your forehead. Your fingers naturally begin to point upward—out through the crown of your head, and continuing without strain up toward the sky. Finally, release your hands, extending your arms out to the side and back down in a circular fashion, and rest your palms on top of your tantien center.

As you do this movement, visualize a golden thread or light inside your body connecting your three centers. Think of your hands as tracing its upward path through your centers and then up and out of the top of your head. Or you can imagine a string of pearls moving through the three centers of your body. Supple yet straight, vivid and luminescent, the string of pearls hangs with perfect verticality right smack dab in the body's center, like a plumb line directed at the earth's center. Now visualize the string extending past the crown of your head to the sky and down past your tailbone to the ground. Follow the string of pearls and feel the inner lift. It feels good, doesn't it?

Sandra, another one of my clients, is a partner in a prominent Washington law firm. Having grown up at a time when women in the workforce were invariably secretaries, she still had trouble believing that she really was a major player in an important arena. The prospect of meetings with CEOs and political heavyweights used to make her break out in a cold sweat, and she felt that she was in over her head. It was instantly clear to me that Sandra wasn't centered; that's why it was so easy to topple her over into insecurity and give her sweaty palms. I suggested a simple solution, an exercise Sandra could do in meetings. Anytime she's in an anxiety-producing situation, she just drops her hands down below the edge of the conference table and places them over her tantien center. It's a simple motion that acts as a trigger, reminding Sandra to get and stay centered. The exercise worked, and the effect has been profound.

Obviously, you can't be centered all the time. Life has a way of coming up with surprises, and some of those surprises can topple you off center. The point is to know how to return to center. That way, you stumble only momentarily, and can remain centered much of the time. Once you know that you can find your way back to your center, you'll also find that it becomes easier to take risks.

Here's another good centering exercise. I've been doing it as I write this book because it helps me think more clearly and focus more sharply. Sit with your back straight, but relaxed. Close your eyes, and visualize a light that starts at your tantien center and extends up to the crown of your head. See it as a bright beam that's swinging from side to side. Let your upper body follow the swinging motion. Like an upside-down pendulum, the size of the swing will diminish over time, so shorten your swinging motion as well. Finally, the beam of light comes to rest as a slim, straight light at your core, and your body stops its movement. See the light and feel its vibration. Breathe fully and deeply, and concentrate on it for several minutes, aware that the source of the light comes from your tantien center. Now you're clear and focused—just let anybody try to nudge you off center!

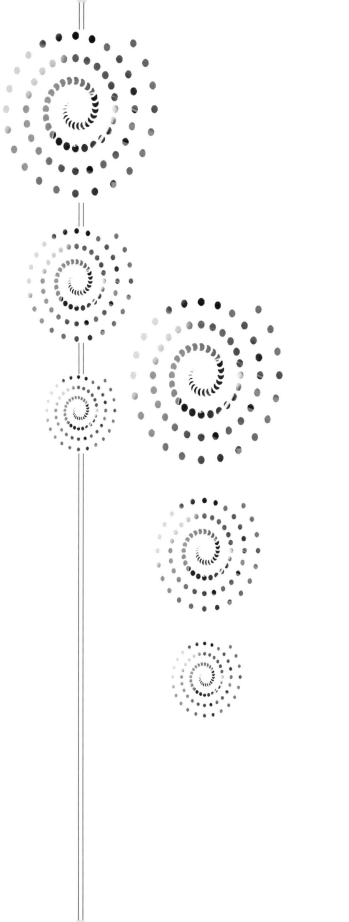

Part II

Bodymind Exercises to Transform Your Life

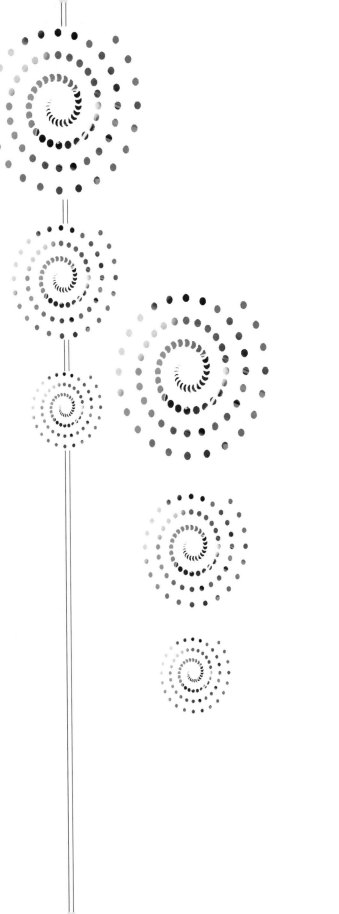

Chapter Four

Everything You Need to Know about the Moving Affirmations

"I find the great thing in this world

is not so much where we stand,

as in what direction we are moving."

— Oliver Wendell Holmes

 you ready to start moving?

In this part of the book, you'll find out how to do the ten Moving Affirmations—the core of the movement practice through which you can begin to heal your life. In these pages, you'll learn what the Moving Affirmations are about, and you'll be given some guidelines as to how to approach them. Then come the step-by-step instructions (with photographs) that show you how to do each of the movements. Later, in Part III, you'll learn which of the Moving Affirmations apply to the specific life issues you want to deal with. You can refer back to this chapter to find the words and pictures that instruct you exactly how to perform the prescribed movement and make the changes you desire.

In addition to the ten basic Moving Affirmation exercises in this chapter, in Chapters 11 and 12 I'll guide you through some exercises intended to be done with another person. These partner exercises can help you heal and strengthen your relationship with your spouse or significant other, and they can be used to stir the passion of an intimate relationship and enhance your pleasure in that passion. The partner exercises can also be used to heal or deepen a friendship or a parent-child relationship, and to create the kind of teamwork that can make any group more productive and successful.

The Moving Affirmations in this chapter, by contrast, provide you with the opportunity to deal with your own personal issues. When you perform a Moving Affirmation, your body is (figuratively) the change you want to see. As you continue to express that change with your body, the effects ripple outward to your awareness and then to your behavior. You'll become more conscious of the choices you're making, and more ready to make alterations in your day-to-day life. Doing these movements will guide you to retrieve your own affirmations from within.

Movement As Therapy: Putting It All in Motion

Here's what the ten Moving Affirmations at the heart of this movement practice are all about.

1. **Step Out of the Box, Open Your Heart and Mind:** Open your perspective and feelings to possibilities that you didn't know existed, gaining lateral thinking and a compassionate heart. You had blinders on and were bound by self-created limitations; this movement takes the blinders off and frees you.

2. **Sky and Earth:** Reach up for the boundless while keeping a firm footing on the ground. Learn to balance sky and earth: If you're too much in the earth, you can get stuck in the mud, but if you're only in the clouds, you'll float aimlessly. With both in balance, everything is possible.

3. **Fire:** Ignite your passion, reclaim your vitality, and turn on your creativity.

4. **Water:** Release tension and stress so you can flow with life.

5. **Wood:** Combine strength and flexibility. From a strong and stable trunk, you can branch out gracefully to explore the world—without being toppled over.

6. **Gold:** Connect with your essential value (the best part of who you are), and know what's most important in your life.

7. **Flight of the Eagle:** Let go of those things that hold you back. Feel free and unencumbered.

8. **Golden Lotus:** Get in touch with your wisdom and inner beauty.

9. **Embrace Tiger:** Accept your ability to handle all that life offers you.

10. **Return to Mountain:** Equipped with a wider perspective, you come home to yourself and become the person you've always wanted to be.

Flip the pages quickly to view a performance of the entire sequence of Moving Affirmations.

"Nothing is more revealing than movement," said the great choreographer and dancer Martha Graham[3]—a dictum I've seen proven in action over and over again. No matter whether an individual knows what a movement is called, whether she has learned what a particular Moving Affirmation is "supposed" to demonstrate, the saying still holds true: If something is off center in a person's life, it will show up in movement. Some part of a sequence will be overemphasized, while another part is underemphasized, or something will consistently be forgotten. Doing the movements becomes a window into the body's wisdom—it's the bodymind's way of sending a message about an imbalance in our lives.

That's why the first time a student comes to my studio, I always begin by asking ask her to go through the entire sequence of Moving Affirmations with me. We keep repeating this sequence together until the student becomes comfortable with it. Then I observe the student. Without fail, my observations give me some clue as to what's happening in the student's inner life. The reason? Our bodies show us not just *where* we've strayed from the real us, but how far and in what direction.

EVERYTHING YOU NEED TO KNOW

The first movement in the sequence of Moving Affirmations asks the student to step out of the box and open her heart and mind. From a standing position, with her hands crossed over her heart, the individual performing this movement will simply step back with either foot, uncross her hands, and open her arms horizontally outward from her body, extending them out past the shoulders. It's as if she's been inside herself, standing straight, with one hand over the other like a ribbon enclosing a package. Now, in one simple movement, she opens the package—body, heart, and mind.

I had a student named Tanya do the Step Out of the Box, Open Your Heart and Mind movement the very first time she came to my studio. But something in the way she did it was instantly, dramatically noticeable: She didn't just open her arms, she flung them out so wide and so hard that her chest jutted forward quite unnaturally, past any point of normal alignment. I was immediately struck by the conspicuous forward thrust of her body, so I asked Tanya if she ever found that she gave herself away in her relationships with men, only to be taken advantage of in the end.

The question stunned her. "All the time," she admitted. "It's a major problem in my life. I know I do it, but I can't seem to fix it."

"Look at yourself as you do this movement," I said, suggesting to Tanya that her extreme way of physically opening up was a reflection of the way she presented herself in a relationship. It was a presentation that would virtually invite her to be taken advantage of, exploited, misused, and even possibly abused. What Tanya's body told me—and what it no doubt told the men she attracted—was that she was ready to give herself away entirely in a relationship, that she would yield herself totally, and that she was almost asking to be wounded.

Together, Tanya and I worked on doing the movement in a more relaxed, natural way—uncrossing her hands gently and extending her arms moderately, in a kind of sliding motion. She did the movement that way every day for a number of weeks. With each passing week, she grew more comfortable, and the physical movement grew more relaxed, until, at a kinesthetic level, she was entirely at ease in not giving herself away. Soon she found that the men who had been drawn to her in the past (who were aggressive, manipulative, highhanded, or exploitive) were no longer interested in her, and she began to attract kinder, gentler men.

Before doing the Moving Affirmation, Tanya had been cognizant of her problem on a rational and intellectual level, but seeing its physical manifestation was what brought her real awareness. Changing the way she moved is what ultimately addressed the problem and led to a highly desirable life change.

. . . ' . . .

As you go through the ten Moving Affirmations, you may be surprised by what you learn about yourself. Or perhaps, like Tanya, you already know what your issue is, where your problem lies, and which challenge you need to overcome. Whatever the case, when you address your issue of the moment, you'll actually be performing three actions all at once. As I mentioned in Chapter 1, you will:

- **intend** a positive desired outcome;
- **affirm** the change you're seeking through a word or phrase; and
- **move** your body as instructed for the particular issue.

An optional fourth step is to **visualize** an image associated with the movement.

The intentions and affirmations that accompany each Moving Affirmation will be found in the separate chapters devoted to specific life issues, since they're tailored to each challenge or problem. What's more, you'll most likely deal with different aspects of an issue at different times in your life, and each aspect may call for different intentions and affirmations. In all cases, I recommend that you develop your own intentions, affirmations, and visualizations. The ones I offer here are meant to guide you to find your own—as in time you will. But the movements themselves don't change.

The Exercises: Getting Ready

"What should I wear to do the movements? Where should I do them, and at what time of day? How long should an exercise session last?" These are the usual questions to ask whenever you start an exercise program, and they deserve to be answered—even though these exercises are aimed not at toning your muscles (although over time, they will), but at bringing about change to the bodymind.

Wear whatever is comfortable. If it's your desire to go out and buy a designer tracksuit to do your Moving Affirmations, then go ahead. If you'd rather wear a torn T-shirt and a pair of sweatpants, that's fine, too. Comfort rules.

The same goes for footwear, although going barefoot or just wearing a pair of socks lets you have closer contact with the floor—a good basis for feeling grounded. But since the aim is to be relaxed from head to toe, dress your feet in whatever achieves that goal. I spent several years doing my Moving Affirmations in platform sandals. They felt great, and they left my feet free and soft. Now, however, I prefer the feeling of my bare feet on the bamboo floor of my studio.

You may not have a separate studio space that you can devote to your Moving Affirmations. That's fine, because you don't need one. You *do* need some room, though—at least enough for you to extend your arms out and up over your head, perhaps enough to stride forward and back a step or two.

As far as when to do your Moving Affirmations, the best time is whenever you can. Leaping out of bed and into a movement won't make it any more effective than doing it at any other time of day or night, but if that's your preference, then that's when you should do it.

Do your Moving Affirmation until it feels as if it's time to stop, or you don't want to do it anymore, or until it makes you happy. In short, you'll know when it's time to stop a particular movement.

Are you getting the overall picture here? It doesn't matter what you wear, where you are, what hour it is, or how much time you spend on the Moving Affirmations, because they're not about the physical or the external. They're about being with yourself, about getting back to your real inner self, and about effecting change in your life—not beating someone at a sport or achieving your personal best.

Remember Robert from Chapter 1? He's the high-powered executive who dashes into the men's room for a quick "refresher" Moving Affirmation when he begins to feel the pressure of business. Clothing, location, time of day, and amount of time are absolutely immaterial to what he does. What counts is the change he can make to his perspective, feelings, and life—simply by moving.

Some Guidelines

While comfort and relaxation are the only "rules" for doing the Moving Affirmations, there are some guidelines you should keep in mind as you begin the movement practice.

- First, there are no angles, edges, corners, or borders in Tai Ji, and muscles are never stretched taut. So when you bend at the knee, elbow, or any other joint, keep the joints soft; don't make sharply etched geometries. Moves should feel easy and relaxed—not as if you're trying to strike an aesthetically pleasing pose.

- Don't judge yourself. This isn't a contest, it's therapy—a healing process. So don't worry if your version of the movement doesn't look exactly like what you see in the photographs. Precision of form is not a high priority.

- Be gentle, stay relaxed, and remember to breathe. The moment you feel any tension, stop. There can be no benefit where there's pain. It doesn't mean that you're doing anything wrong, it simply means that you should stop doing the exercise the way you're doing it.

- Know your limitations, but don't feel limited. I once worked with a student who had no arms, yet his intentions stretched his body up to the sky and down to the earth. It was a vivid demonstration of the power of the bodymind.

- Balance is important. If you begin a movement on your left foot, be sure you do it again starting on your right foot. Again, remember to breathe.

- Let the movements come from your tantien center—the source, origin, and very core of you. Start and end each Moving Affirmation with your hands on your tantien center. Feel the line coming up from the earth, through your three centers (your tantien, heartmind, and third eye), and up to the sky. Think in terms of aligning all three centers rather than "standing up straight"; you should have a sense of lengthening rather than stretching.

In Sequence

In addition to undertaking a stand-alone Moving Affirmation to address a particular issue, you can also learn to do all ten in sequence to provide a holistic sense of harmony and balance in your life. After all, the movement practice in this book is aimed not only at "fixing" a problem, curing an ailment, or remedying a difficulty, but equally at reconnecting, realigning, and rebalancing your life.

When you do all ten Moving Affirmations as a sequence, you don't need to stop at the center after each movement. Instead, pass through the center and continue moving from one movement to another as fluidly and naturally as you can. You can refer to the photos in Appendix C to help you flow through this sequence.

You may be eager to address the specific life issue or issues that concern you at this moment, but I recommend that, in due course, you practice the total sequence. I start each day by going through all ten, consciously, joyously, and as fluidly as possible. Not surprisingly, after decades of practice, my morning routine has become quite fluent indeed.

And while, for me, going through the Moving Affirmations is a habit as automatic as putting on a seat belt in my car, I try to focus intently on what I'm doing as I do it.

At the very least, the sequence provides a respite from the day's stresses and strains, replacing them with a sense of calm and strength—but it can do so much more. When you do the ten Moving Affirmations as a sequence, all of the movements become reminders of how you want to be in life: open to possibilities, connected to nature, and flowing with the currents that run within and outside you. They remind you that you're not alone, you're part of a bigger picture, you have passion and vitality within you if you know how to stir them, and that there are no limits to your possibilities if you just look at them in a fresh way. If you're feeling uncertain, then doing the movements gives you the sense of support you need to go on. If you're feeling disconnected, they give you a safe way to connect. Likewise, if you're stressed, you can turn on the movements the way you might turn on a shower, and let your tension and discontent wash away.

Each of the Moving Affirmations reminds you of what's within and lets you bring it out. As you move through life's twists and turns, they are there to summon as needed, so you can return to the essence of yourself and fully realize your potential.

Are you ready? Then go for it!

Every Move You Make

Instructions for the Moving Affirmations

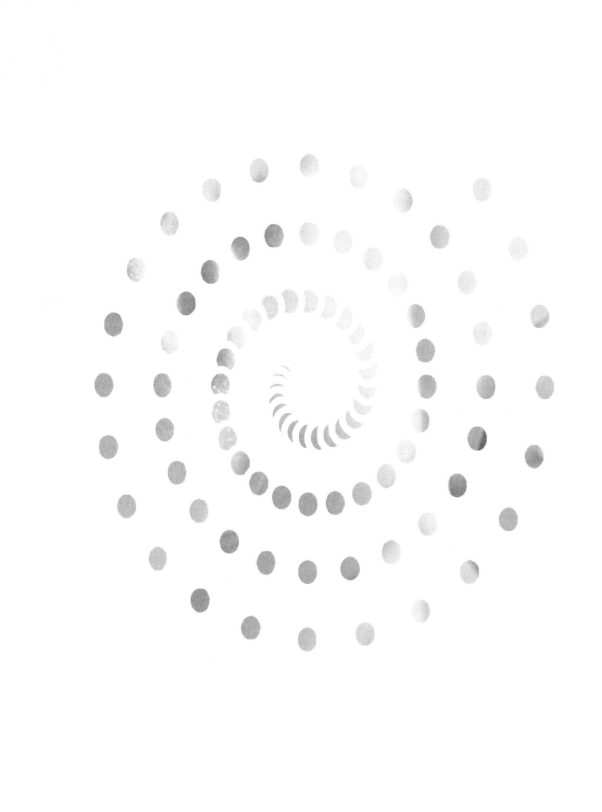

Step Out of the Box,
Open Your Heart and Mind

Preview of Complete Movement

Step-by-Step

(a) First Move

(b) Second Move

(c) Third Move

(d) Fourth Move

(e) Final Move

Instructions for Step Out of the Box, Open Your Heart and Mind

(a) Stand with all three of your centers (tantien, heartmind, and third eye) aligned. You should be relaxed and comfortable with your legs parallel, approximately hip-width apart, and your knees soft.

(b) Bring your hands up in front of your face, with your palms turned toward your face and wrists crossed.

(c) Step back on your left foot. This is the yin foot—the passive, receptive, cosmic principle—so prepare yourself to receive. Balance evenly on both feet.

(d) In a smooth and relaxed fashion, open your arms outward. Open the fingers of your hands, open your eyes, feel your throat open, and let your heart and mind open. Take your time, and continue opening up and receiving. Do this movement several times if you wish.

(e) When you feel fully open to the world's possibilities, bring your left foot back to where it was, and, as you'll do at the end of every movement, bring your hands back to your tantien center.

Do the movement again—this time starting with your right foot back and left foot forward. This is the yang foot—the active, assertive principle—which helps you gain balance and put into motion the new possibilities you've come to see. (But don't expect any dramatic changes overnight; while you may see them right away, it could take time.)

As you do this movement, you might imagine yourself clearing the morning fog, or perhaps opening sparkling beaded curtains to a new adventure. See your mind expanding and feel your heart opening.

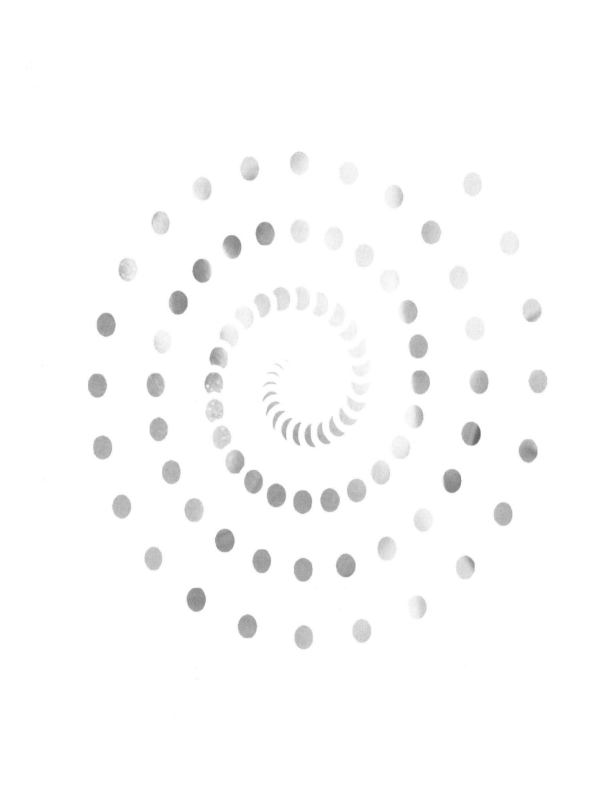

Sky and Earth

Preview of Complete Movement

Step-by-Step

(a) First Move

(b) Second Move

Side View

(c) Third Move

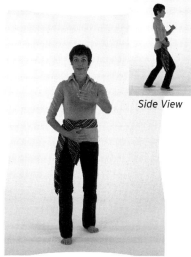

Side View

(d) Fourth Move

Side View

(e) Fifth Move

Side View

(f) Final Move

Instructions for Sky and Earth

(a) Stand with your left foot back, right foot forward, and weight balanced evenly.

(b) Now your right arm goes down and your left arm goes up. Your rising arm connects you to sky, while the arm reaching down connects you to earth, but it's up to you which direction you'll reach for first. (For example, if you're feeling "stuck in the mud," first raise your left arm to the sky so you can "lighten up," then reach down with your right arm. Likewise, if you're feeling out of touch with reality, go to earth with your left arm to get the grounding you need before your reach up with your right arm. If you're not sure how you feel, then clear your mind and let your body lead you—or raise and lower both arms simultaneously.) Your palms are open and your fingertips are extended.

Take a moment to think about the energy of the earth coming up through you and the energy of the sky coming down through you. Imagine a wire connecting your three centers and conducting energy in free-flowing channels up and down your body. Remember: You're not trying to stretch as high as possible, but rather to open the channels within, so that the energies of sky and earth can flow freely, dissolving all blockages.

(c) (d) (e) (f) Bring your arms together, looping them toward the center simultaneously—as if gathering in the energies they represent. Your sky arm circles down and in toward your body, while your earth arm circles out and up; the arms loop over one another and come back to center together. Step forward with your left foot so that both feet are parallel.

As you do these gathering motions, think about bringing the two energies—the stable, nurturing, receptive energy of mother earth, and the inspirational, no-boundaries, assertive energy of father sky—back into balance in your body.

Do the movement again, this time starting with your right foot back and left foot forward. Remember to alternate the position of your arms as well.

As you do this exercise, picture the abundance of the heavens opening to you and pouring into your body. Feel the depth and support of the powerful earth moving up through you to your tantien center.

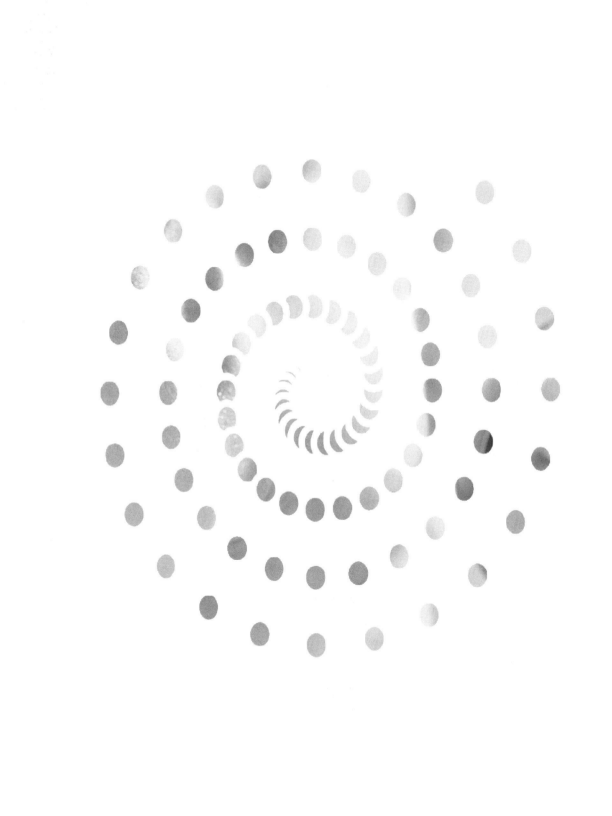

Fire

Preview of Complete Movement

Step-by-Step

(a) First Move

(b) Second Move

(c) Third Move

(d) Fourth Move

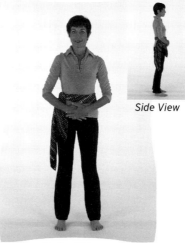

(e) Final Move

Instructions for Fire

(a) Start with your left foot back, right foot forward, and weight balanced evenly. Your hands should be at the tantien level on either side of your hips.

Imagine that a force—a celestial hand—is pushing into the small of your back. Sense energy moving into the base of your spine and then forward out of your tantien.

Open your hands at tantien level on either side of your hips; let them guide the fire outward. Your palms should be facing one another with your fingers open, almost as if you just drew a pair of six-shooters. Rest them lightly against your hips and keep both legs soft at the knees.

(b) (c) Shift your weight from your back leg until it's mostly on your front leg, with your back leg forming an almost-straight line. Don't move your feet, though; only your weight moves as you take your body forward and feel your vitality, passion, and fire ignited.

Move your arms out and forward as if opening the furnace of your inner fire and letting it grow, warm you, and light the world. Extend your arms as far forward as possible, keeping both feet flat and fully connected to the ground without losing your balance. Then raise your arms to let the flame of your own fire rise to the sky above your head.

(d) Shift your weight so that it's evenly distributed over your two legs. Bring your arms back down, and return your hands to your center.

(e) Finally, move your feet back to their parallel position.

Do the movement again—this time starting with your right foot back and left foot forward.

As you do the movement, picture a light or flame moving out from your tantien and being guided by your hands. Feel the sensation.

Water

Preview of Complete Movement

Side View

(a) First Move

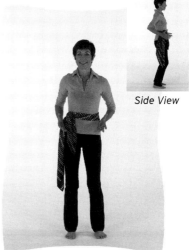

Side View

(b) Second Move

Side View

(c) Third Move

Side View

(d) Fourth Move

(e) Fifth Move

(f) Sixth Move

(g) Seventh Move

Side View

(h) Final Move

Instructions for Water

(a) Stand with all three of your centers aligned. You should be relaxed and comfortable, with your legs parallel, approximately hip-width apart, and your knees soft.

(b) (c) (d) From your center, circle your arms out in front of you and up toward the sky.
Your palms should be open and facing each other; your fingertips relaxed and reaching for the clouds.

(e) (f) (g) (h) Imagine that you're under a waterfall. Turn your arms into the undulating currents of descending water as you lower them. Imagine the water flowing and rippling in gentle waves—down, down, down—as your arms lower as far as possible without you bending. Feel the water draining out through your fingertips.

Do this movement as many times as you like. Think about the motions: opening up, flowing down, and breathing. Feel it inside, and picture the tensions flowing out of you.
As you do this movement, you might visualize yourself standing under a cool waterfall on a tropical island, with the water flowing over your body to the earth.

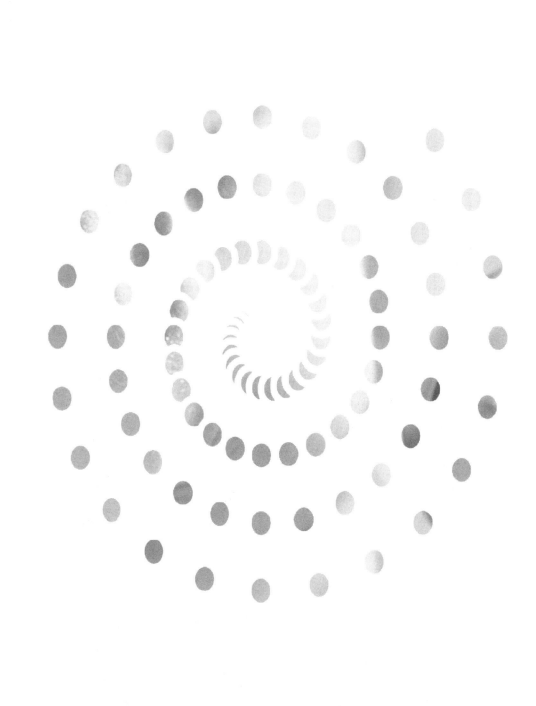

Wood

Preview of Complete Movement

EVERYTHING YOU NEED TO KNOW . . .

Step-by-Step

(a) First Move

(b) Second Move

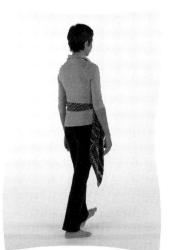

(c) Third Move

(d) Fourth Move

(e) Fifth Move

(f) Sixth Move

(g) Seventh Move

(h) Eighth Move

(i) Ninth Move

(j) Tenth Move

(k) Eleventh Move

(l) Final Move

EVERYTHING YOU NEED TO KNOW . . .

Instructions for Wood

(a) Stand with left foot back, right foot forward, and weight balanced.

(b) (c) Pivot first on your front heel, then on your back heel in the direction your hips are open to. Turn halfway around in the direction you find easiest—this will be the most natural way for you to turn. You are now facing a point 180 degrees from where you started.

(d) (e) Slowly and comfortably extend your arms out in front of your body at shoulder level, moving them out from your center like the branches of a tree. Remember to keep your shoulders relaxed.

(f) (g) (h) (i) (j) (k) (l) With your arms still at shoulder level, begin to move your feet back the way you came, still pivoting, so that you end up where you started. And continue in that direction, stepping smoothly around—centered, relaxed—until you have gone a full 360 degrees. Allow your arms to move slightly as if swaying gently in a breeze. End with both feet parallel, and bring hands back to center.

Do the movement again—this time starting with your right foot back and left foot forward.

As you do this movement, imagine yourself connected to the earth like a dancing tree—rooted, yet swaying gently with the winds; grounded and stable, yet flexible. Notice how your vision opens and expands.

Gold

Step-by-Step

(a) First Move

(b) Second Move

(c) Third Move

(d) Fourth Move

(e) Fifth Move

(f) Sixth Move

Step-by-Step

(g) Seventh Move

(h) Eighth Move

(i) Ninth Move

(j) Tenth Move

(k) Final Move

Instructions for Gold

(a) Stand with all three of your centers aligned. You should be relaxed and comfortable, with your legs parallel, approximately hip-width apart, and your knees soft.

(b) (c) (d) Pivot slowly and gently on your right heel as you open your right hip. At the same time, reach down and out with your right arm and begin to trace a large circle in the air–the globe of the world. The fingers are pointed to the earth and are slightly bent as you circle your arm down, then on the way up, they point toward the sky. Meanwhile, your left hand stays at center throughout, flat or lightly cupped against your tantien; it's your anchor as you pan for your own gold and reach out for the resources you need– those that speak to your own essential value.

Be sure you look where you're reaching–let your eyes move with your arm–so that you can influence what you bring into yourself and not just settle for whatever is out there.

(e) (f) As your arm finishes its circle, your hip returns to the frontal position. Let your arm trace the line down from the crown of your head through your centers and back to tantien. This is the receiving motion: You've opened up to what's out there, and you're bringing your treasure home.

(g) (h) (i) (j) (k) Do the movement again–this time pivoting on your left heel, opening your left hip, and reaching out with your left arm.

As you do this movement, you might picture a golden light moving into your center, then emanating out from it. It reminds you, as you reach for the true riches of the universe, to feel the deep, abiding value of your highest self.

Flight of the Eagle

Preview of Complete Movement

(a) First Move

(b) Second Move

(c) Third Move

(d) Fourth Move

(f) Fifth Move

(f) Sixth Move

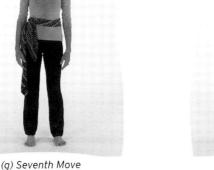

(g) Seventh Move

(h) Final Move

Instructions for Flight of the Eagle

(a) Stand with all three of your centers aligned. You should be relaxed and comfortable, with your legs parallel (approximately hip-width apart), your knees soft, and your hands at center.

Open your hands in front of your center. Imagine that you're holding a weight in your open hands. It's something that's holding you back and weighing you down. Feel the weight, and feel your knees give a bit under the heaviness.

(b) Now let go—you don't have to carry whatever is weighing you down, and you don't need to hold onto whatever is holding your life back. Let your arms fall and simply drop the weight.

(c) (d) (e) (f) (g) (h) Your arms then lift up and out to the sides, as if you're lifting your wings out from under your body—out and up. You're flying. Your palms are open, maybe up, maybe down—whichever feels natural to you at that moment. Soar like the eagle you are. Then come back to center.

Do this movement as many times as you like, but remember: All eagles come home to roost.

As you do this movement, picture yourself as a soaring eagle, flying high into a sunlit sky, above the clouds—peaceful, sublime, and seeing with eagle eyes.

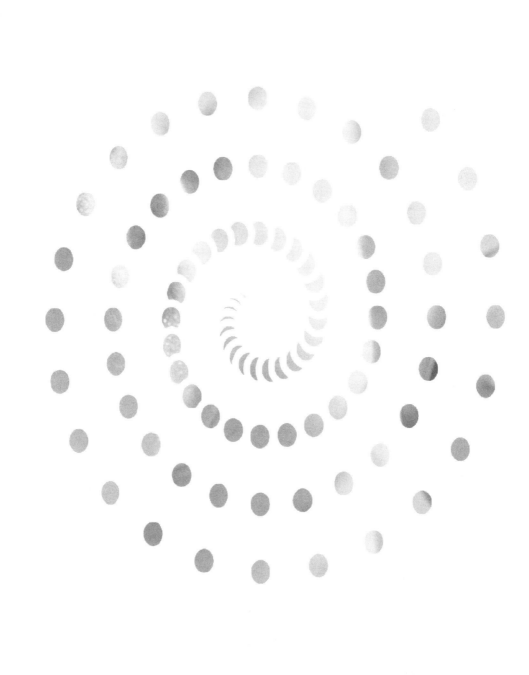

Golden Lotus

Golden Lotus

Preview of Complete Movement

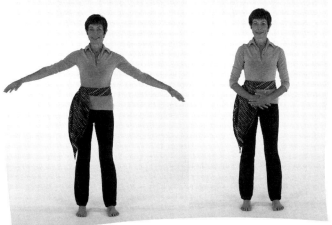

(a) First Move

(b) Second Move

(c) Third Move

(d) Fourth Move

(e) Fifth Move

(f) Sixth Move

(g) Seventh Move

(h) Final Move

Instructions for Golden Lotus

(a) Stand with all three of your centers aligned. You should be relaxed and comfortable, with your legs parallel, approximately hip-width apart, and your knees soft.

(b) Release your arms, soften your knees, and reach down.

(c) (d) (e) (f) Imagine yourself as a flower, bringing earth up through your stem. Let your arms and hands flow up the center line of your body—right up to the crown of your head and beyond.

(g) (h) Now let your arms release out and down both sides of the stem toward the earth, as the flower opens, petal by petal. The Chinese say that the golden lotus has a thousand petals; feel them opening. Then bring your hands back to center.

Do this movement as many times as you need to in order to feel your inner beauty and wisdom flowering.

As you do this movement, you might imagine your body as a stem opening up into a flower of a thousand golden petals that sprout through the top of your head and fall gently over your body.

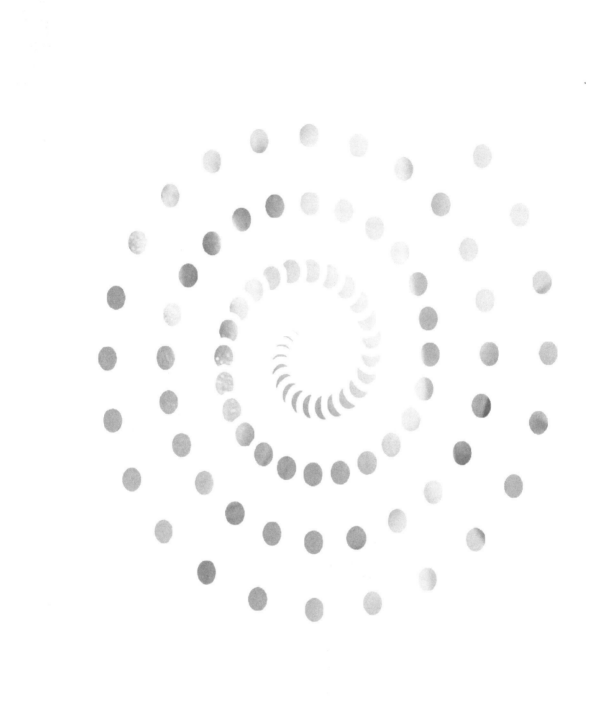

Embrace Tiger

Preview of Complete Movement

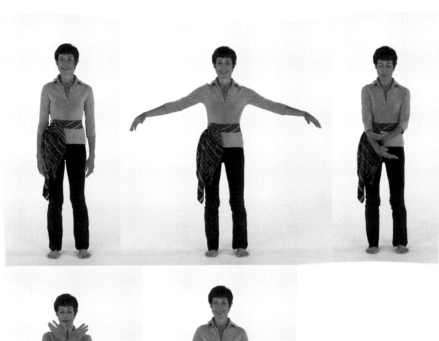

Step-by-Step

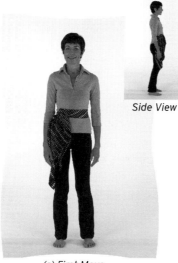

Side View

(a) First Move

Side View

(b) Second Move

Side View

(c) Third Move

Side View

(d) Fourth Move

Side View

(e) Final Move

Instructions for Embrace Tiger

(a) Stand with all three of your centers aligned. You should be relaxed and comfortable, with your legs parallel, approximately hip-width apart, and your knees soft.

(b) (c) First your arms float up, and then, softening your knees, reach down to the earth for the stabilizing energy you need to support you.

(d) You arms cross over each other near the wrists and your hands move up to a point just below eye level. Your palms should be open and toward you, one palm over the other. It doesn't matter which is over which, but when you repeat the movement, alternate. Look at your hands. You're embracing the tiger, and your open palms mean you can look the tiger in the eye. You're looking life in the eye now, equipped to handle all it will offer.

(e) Bring your hands back to center.

As you do this movement, visualize the strength and grace of a single tiger; imagine that he has allowed you to embrace him and to absorb his power into your heart and your entire being.

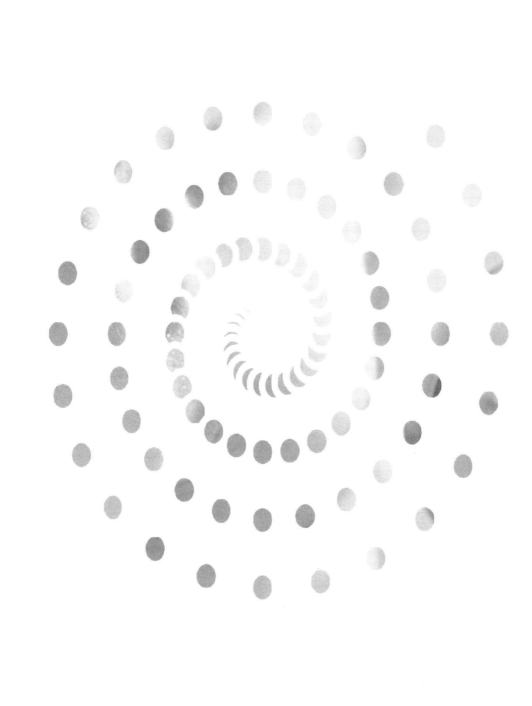

Return to Mountain

Return to Mountain

Preview of Complete Movement

EVERYTHING YOU NEED TO KNOW . . .

Step-by-Step

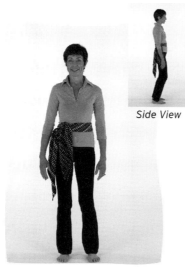

Side View

(a) First Move

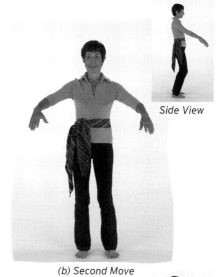

Side View

(b) Second Move

Side View

(c) Third Move

Side View

(d) Fourth Move

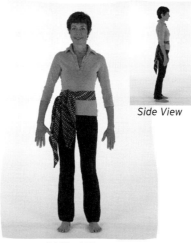

Side View

(e) Final Move

Instructions for Return to Mountain

(a) (b) (c) Relax your arms. Let them float up, up, up as you imagine yourself floating above the summit of a mountain.

(d) (e) Now let your arms float down, soften your knees, and let your palms land softly by your side—like an astronaut landing on the moon. You're home now, with new serenity.

Do this movement as often as you like. Float back up, then down, back up again, and down again—as many times as you wish, wave after wave, until you're ready for a landing. You're grounded and centered, and just this once, you don't even need to bring your hands back to center.

As you do this movement, you might visualize yourself floating down to the top of a mountain. Everything you see is beautiful. Picture yourself coming to your home with a new sense of power and a wider perspective.

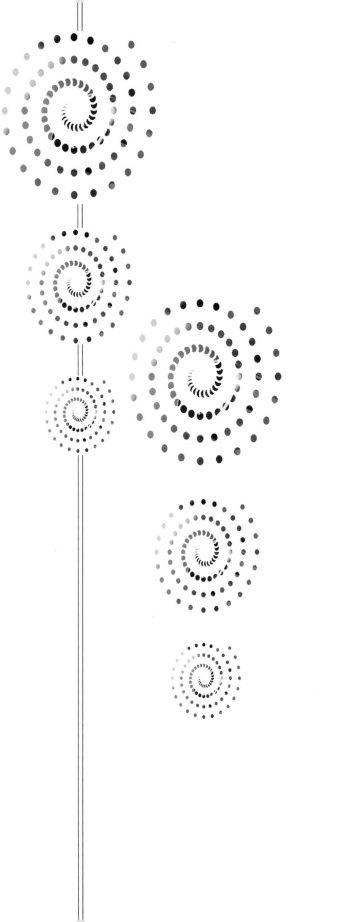

Part III

Moving to Address the Issues in Your Life

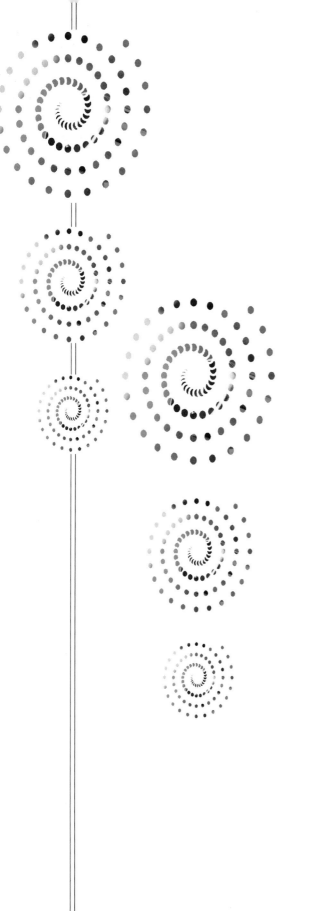

Chapter Five

Breaking Through the Limits of Your Life

"The significant problems we face cannot

be solved at the same level of thinking

we were at when we created them."

—Albert Einstein

Picture

Picture an exotic tropical locale (exotic back-drops are almost always tropical, it seems). Find yourself in the slightly dilapidated capital city of this location, in an intriguing bar on a narrow street. You're seated at a small round table, drinking the local specialty. The place is dark, offering respite from the sun's heat, and overhead fans whir, moving the air ever so slightly. You hear music coming from the next room—a slow, rhythmic, seductive melody. Mixed in with the strains is a bright, tinkling sound coming from the beaded curtain that serves as the doorway to the next room. The slightest breeze, even from the overhead fan, disturbs the curtain and stirs its chiming sound, and the beaded strands catch the light and sparkle as they jangle and clink. You can tell that something's going on behind that veiled opening, but the movement, the glitter, and the light blur your view.

Step Out of the Box, Open Your Heart and Mind is the first step toward parting the curtain and seeing what really lies behind it. It's the Moving Affirmation that will free you and open you up to limitless new possibilities. The "box" you need to step out of is the problem for which you can find no solution, the circumstance begging for some kind of remedy, or the life situation that fills you with malaise. Perhaps you feel as if you're stuck and there's no way out. You know that something's wrong, but there's nothing you can do about it. Or maybe you've told yourself, "That's just life."

But the truth is, all the changes you want to make start when you break through the self-limiting patterns that have been weighing down your life. When you practice this Moving Affirmation, you'll begin to see the world with fresh eyes, and open your heart and mind to choices, alternatives, and options you never knew existed—whether they relate to your career, relationships, or personal well-being.

How Did I Get Here?

Maybe you fell into the box you're in. It happens—life is full of traps, and it's all too human to drop into one. Maybe the hobby that once seemed like the world's most exciting pursuit has grown tedious through repetition, a long-term relationship has become more of a habit than a commitment, or it could be that the career you spent years building has turned out to be much less fulfilling than you had assumed.

More often than not, we build the boxes in which we find ourselves, brick by brick, over time. Take, for example, the case of my client Diana. In a contentious custody battle with her ex-husband, Diana staked out a take-no-prisoners position. Her ex wanted equal time

with their daughter, but Diana insisted on being granted more than her former husband—and she wanted the disparity in her favor noted in the legal custody agreement. In fact, it was hard to tell which she wanted more—time with her daughter, or a triumph over her ex-husband. Her instructions to her lawyer were unequivocal: There was to be no retreat, not an inch. That's how Diana defined winning.

But in truth, she was losing. She was so focused on the battle, so locked into the fight, that she couldn't move beyond it. All she could do was take the same action over and over, deliver the same demand, and reject anything short of it. Not surprisingly, the result was the same each time, too: deadlock, and a continuing battle.

The Diana who came to my studio one summer morning was an articulate, attractive woman who combined an outgoing charm with an aura of competence and command. She was conscientious and deliberate in everything she did—from the way she listened to my instruction to the way she prepared herself to, as she said, "run through the exercise." As I talked her through the Moving Affirmation for Step Out of the Box, she stood straight and relaxed in her new leotard and sweatshirt. She brought her hands up in front of her face, palms facing in. But when I asked her to step back on her left (yin) foot, something happened. Diana was suddenly stuck. She didn't actually step back at all—she simply skipped right past that motion, as if it had nothing to do with her.

To me, this was a clear sign that Diana simply wasn't able to widen her perspective, and it betrayed her predicament right away: If she stayed in the same spot, she'd keep on seeing the same thing—over and over and over. A moment later, when the movement called for Diana to open her arms, she pushed outward instead, as if she were trying to push the situation away. Of course, that's just what she wanted to do—make the whole thing disappear.

Caught in a box, Diana could see nothing beyond its walls, and no real possibilities for action. True, Diana had built this box herself, piling anger on top of bitterness on top of resentment on top of disillusionment. But that didn't make its walls any easier to see through. Since she was unable to perceive options, all that was left for her was to wish that the problem would evaporate—and of course, it wouldn't without action by her. She was caught in a vicious circle: She couldn't move because she couldn't see anywhere to move to; she couldn't see because she was stuck in one place. If Diana was ever going to get past her anger and her need to "win," she was going to have to climb out of that box, look at life through a wider lens, open her heart to kinder feelings, and unlock her mind to fresh options.

In time—in fact, after only a week of our work together—Diana consciously changed both her "missteps," and her outlook shifted markedly. As she learned to step back and open her arms, she quickly began to see possibilities beyond her unflinching instructions to her lawyer. She began to understand that her struggle was costing her more than any so-called victory was worth. She had a new understanding.

Clearing the Fog

The goal of this Moving Affirmation—Step Out of the Box, Open Your Heart and Mind—is that you gain a wider perspective. The reason you can't move when you're in a box is because you can't see *where* to move; in fact, when you're inside, you can't actually see the box. You don't know that you're enclosed because you think the box is all there is—and if the box is all you can see, boxed-in emotions are all you'll feel.

When the San Francisco Bay is wrapped in a blanket of its famous fog, you can't distinguish sea from land; you can drive across the Golden Gate without even knowing you're on a bridge. All you see—and all you know—is a few feet of road illuminated by your headlights. City, bay, and bridge might as well not exist. But Step Out of the Box, Open Your Heart and Mind clears your life's fog from your eyes and shows you all the roads that stretch out around you.

A Simple Shift

You don't need to begin your journey like a bull in a china shop—you don't need to kick down the walls of the box or smash them to smithereens. The movement really is a matter of a single step outside the walls to a place where your vision is unlimited, so that you can open your life to limitless potential.

That's a lesson that Maureen, a powerful business executive, learned from her sessions with me. At the time, she managed significant profit-and-loss responsibility and commanded substantial budgetary and personnel resources. She also served on the executive policy committee and was considered the organization's key public relations point person. She was extremely influential and well compensated, she traveled widely, and she always flew first class.

Anyone would have said that she had it all. But Maureen still wanted to rise higher. She craved the company's top job with an all-consuming appetite. She'd been part of this organization her entire working life. She'd given it her all, and she'd almost literally made it her life. Getting to the top of it was the ultimate aim—what else was there?

The fact of the matter was that Maureen had hit her personal ceiling in the company; she simply wasn't in contention for the top job she wanted. But she didn't see it. In her eyes, she simply hadn't found the way to the top yet—and the top was all that she fixed her gaze on; it was all she wanted.

So she kept striving. She wasn't only in a box; she was on a treadmill in the box! But Maureen was running so fast that it was difficult to see that she wasn't advancing. She forgot that on a treadmill, it's the *track* that moves—she was just running in place on a path going nowhere.

I could see the issue reflected in Maureen's movements. When she opened her arms in Step Out of the Box, she opened them just so far and no farther; as if she were unfolding only the middle 10 feet of shutters on a 30-foot-wide picture window. We began to work on widening Maureen's arms *and* her view, enough so that she could see lots of possibilities and an answer to, "What else is there besides rising to the top in the company?" Over the course of a year, Maureen's options seemed to constantly multiply as her perspective continued to stretch. After a year, Maureen did something she never would have thought possible before: She left the company that had been her life and started her own consulting enterprise. Her field of expertise? Helping corporations develop wider perspectives and lateral thinking—the very thing that had been her own life issue became the core of her new and highly successful livelihood.

∙ ∙ ∙ ' ∙ ∙ ∙

David's story also reflects the concept that a simple shift in perspective can open your life up to new possibilities. David was young, nice-looking, single, and independent when he came to me for lessons. He had recently quit a job that had brought him more headaches than satisfaction. It had been an interesting occupation, and he was certainly the right person for it, but a grinding daily commute and the entanglements of office politics had poisoned his workday every day. Now he had some money in his pocket, no immediate responsibilities, and time to search for the perfect opportunity that would advance his career smoothly along the fast track. It was the first time in his life that he hadn't worked, and he was enjoying having no agenda at all—at least, he said he was.

But when it came time for him to do this particular Moving Affirmation, he found it very difficult to open his arms. When I urged him to get past his limited vision and open his arms outward, he began to push with his hands, as if he were rejecting the possibilities that were out there. David was confined—not by the traffic on his route to work, but by his own inability to see beyond his normal perceptions and receive what he might find. He was boxed in to a way of life that his body movements made clear wasn't satisfying to him.

David and I practiced embracing armloads of possibilities, not thrusting them away. "Think about what *you* want," I advised him. And when the company asked David to come back, his answer was neither a yes nor a no, but something else altogether—an entirely new arrangement, the sort of thing David had never thought of doing before. He asked for a four-day week, two of which he'd work from home. He asked for specific changes in the nature of the projects he was assigned to, and he asked for more money.

You know what? He got it all. He'd been so caught up in the company's world that he couldn't see beyond it. Learning to embrace more possibilities and using that as a springboard to think about what he wanted, David was able to articulate a career that was his choice—and get it.

You create the life you believe you've always wanted—and then you feel trapped in it. You tell yourself that maturity means accepting some unvarnished basic truths: Work can't always be great; grand passion isn't sustainable; mortgages must be paid; if disappointment is part of life, so is learning to put up with it. This is "the way life is"; it's not going to change. *Life* is the box we're in.

No, it isn't. Life is what's behind the beaded curtain; it's what you can see when the fog clears. That's why stepping out of the box and opening your heart and mind are essential first steps toward transforming your life. They make it possible for you to *see*—that you're in a box, that there are other options, that life can be different, that you can walk through that beaded curtain and embrace life's possibilities, and that you're *ready* to do so.

So begin.

Intend

- *I intend to find the solution to the [fill in the blank] problem in my life.*
- *I intend to let go of self-imposed limitations.*

Affirm

- *I am open to new possibilities.*
- *I am open to new solutions.*

Move

- *Step Out of the Box, Open the Heart and Mind*

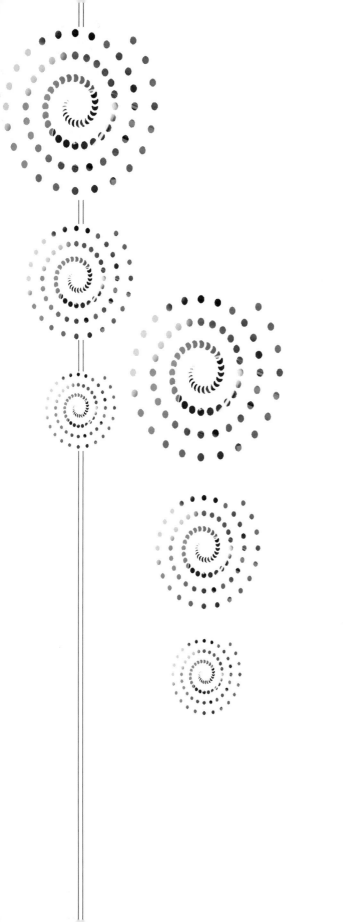

Chapter Six

Dancing Your Own Dance: Becoming the Authentic You

". . . as we let our own light shine,

we unconsciously give other people

permission to do the same. As we are

liberated from our own fear, our

presence automatically liberates others."

— Marianne Williamson[4]

If you watch a small child dance, you'll notice that it's the most natural thing in the world. With absolute abandon—that is, without shyness, nervousness, or self-consciousness about people watching—kids just move to the music as their bodies command. Yes, this is proof that dance movements are basic and universal, but it should also remind you of how far you may have come from your natural-movement origins. After all, do you dance that way today? Maybe in the privacy of your bedroom, where you can assure yourself that no one is watching, but on the public dance floor you're doing steps you've learned—dances choreographed by popular culture or social norms or copied from movies, magazines, and television. It's as if your basic dance instincts—the movements you did as a child—have been "educated" out of you.

Unfortunately, that may be a measure of how far you've traveled from the real you. Trying to be somebody or something you're not—dancing someone else's dance—is exhausting, wasteful, and doomed to ultimate failure. You won't be able to pull it off, but you'll expend vast amounts of time and energy trying—a costly effort for minimal return.

You are who and what you are. As Marianne Williamson, author of numerous best-selling books on personal growth, wrote, you have your own "light," or your own potential to be "brilliant, gorgeous, talented, and fabulous." When you feel confident about your identity, secure in your self-image, and assured of your authenticity, you'll realize that what you have to say ought to be heard, what you're feeling is worth feeling, and your actions should reflect your convictions and beliefs. The alternative is wasting your life by trying to fit into somebody else's idea of who you are.

The focus of three of the Moving Affirmations is to help you find, feel, and be yourself: Fire teaches you to "let your own light shine"; Golden Lotus opens you to your highest potential; Sky and Earth boosts your self confidence.

Do You Dare? Fire and Golden Lotus Movements

Tracy was a woman who always felt inadequate and never quite believed in her own inner light. She was everybody's handmaiden, best pal, and support system—and she was good at it. As the only girl in a family of brilliant brothers, she had, in a sense, been trained for a secondary role. What's more, her extended family was filled with renowned artists, writers, and musicians. All her life, Tracy had been encouraged to feel grateful to bring these celebrity relatives a glass of water, fetch them something they needed, or praise their efforts and applaud their achievements.

Not surprisingly, given the circles in which she moved, Tracy married a well-known set designer who was in demand both in Hollywood and on Broadway. What was also no surprise was that she prided herself on serving as *his* personal support system—she was attuned to every nuance and shift in his artistic temperament, and was ready to minister to his every need.

She basically did the same thing for her friends. She was a patient listener, available at any hour of day or night. She was there to take care of kids or animals, act as a car service, and offer advice or help when it was needed.

As for her own talents, Tracy was quick to insist that she had none. Her ability, she'd claim, lay in propping up others. Reared to expect little of herself, Tracy was always ready to stop short when it came to living her own identity. She simply didn't allow herself to believe that she had other abilities, or a role to play other than "useful subordinate."

Yet there must have been some feeling of being off center in that role, because Tracy was eager to begin my movement practice. As we went through the sequence of Moving Affirmations together, two movements in particular made Tracy's self-image issues evident.

First, when she first did the Fire movement, there was almost no energy—even Tracy described her attempt as "wimpy." I suggested that she use the Fire movement to help ignite her passion and shine her light into the world, but she said that she didn't feel it was okay to shine or follow her passion—she was afraid that it might undermine someone else. But after further discussion, Tracy decided that by shining her light, she could perhaps help others do the same. Marianne Williamson wrote: "There is nothing enlightened about shrinking so that other people won't feel insecure around you." Once Tracy understood that, her intention and affirmation came easily:

Intend

- *I intend to share my light and my passion with the world.*

Affirm

- *I have my own gifts to share with people.*

Move

- *Fire*

The second movement that was off balance in Tracy was the Golden Lotus movement. When I asked her to move her arms up through her body's three centers toward the sky and let her hands spread open like the petals of a flower, Tracy stopped short. Her arms lumbered tentatively somewhere in the vicinity of her head, and her hands never opened at all.

As is my habit, I told Tracy what I saw and asked her, "What about your talents?"

Tracy shook her head and said, "I really don't have any special abilities." She still didn't dare believe that she had her own gifts.

"Would you be willing to be open to them?"

Tracy considered the question, shrugged, and finally said, "Yes."

I asked Tracy to create her own intention for doing the Golden Lotus movement. It was: "I intend to be all that I can be." We worked on the movement together, visualizing a flower growing high and opening fully. That's what Tracy focused on as she brought her hands up through her center toward the sky—higher than she'd ever gone before. Finger by finger, her hands opened completely, like the petals of a flower. She said it felt as if her whole body was opening up. Her affirmation as she did the movement? "I dare to reach for my dreams."

To Tracy's own surprise, that's exactly what she did. When she found her dreams— dreams she hadn't even known she had—she discovered who she really was. It was a revelation. She had always known that she was good at supporting others, what she now learned was that she also had unique talents that could be developed—in fact, she's now writing a book about a famous member of her family. Tracy has reclaimed herself as a woman whose abilities match her dreams. She still does the Golden Lotus movement each day, and still reaches ever higher—for the next dream, and for the full flowering of her talents and abilities.

Try it:

Intend

- *I intend to be all that I can be.*

Affirm

- *I dare to reach for my dreams.*

Move

- *Golden Lotus*

Whose Life Is It Anyway? Sky and Earth Movement

Melinda seemed to be a poised, "with-it" woman. She was tall, attractive, and athletic-looking. Yet she completely lacked confidence both in herself and in her own thoughts and beliefs. She went whichever way the wind blew, wavered in all her decisions, and let others dictate her beliefs. She even joked about it: "I listen to a debate the way I watch tennis," she told me. "I'm absolutely convinced by both opposing arguments."

In plans, projects, and even leisure activities, Melinda always let others have their way—"to avoid problems," she said, "and to keep things uncomplicated." Of course it was uncomplicated: Lacking the courage of her own convictions, Melinda simply yielded to everybody else's. When we did the Moving Affirmations sequence together, Melinda's long back seemed to sway and bend, as if her spine were giving way under unseen pressure. It was the physical manifestation of her insecurity about herself, a reflection of her lack of resolution, of her feeling that she didn't deserve to have her way. Melinda lacked backbone.

The issue was particularly important because Melinda was preparing to go into business with two other people. From the outset, the business had been based on Melinda's concept and contacts, yet she doubted her ability to do it alone. So she invited her friend Janice, who had also trained as a graphic designer, to join her in opening a Website design studio. Melinda assumed it just "made sense," as she put it, to cede most of the business decision-making to Janice's husband, Tom, a senior manager at a bank; after all, he was a businessman and an expert in finance. Along the way, however, Melinda began to realize that Tom and Janice were minimizing Melinda's position in the embryonic business, rejecting her ideas and vetoing her suggestions. The business she had conceived was becoming *their* business, and her dream was being eroded. Soon, the business plan looked nothing like what Melinda had envisioned: Tom and Janice were in charge, and they were going to reap most of the financial rewards.

That long, yielding spine was the physical manifestation of the Melinda who never even considered that she could speak up for herself in negotiations with Tom and Janice, or perhaps reconsider whether this partnership was the right thing. So she and I set about strengthening her spine.

The idea was to make Melinda feel more empowered, and the tool we used was the Sky and Earth movement. In Melinda's case, the arm reaching for the sky represented her reach for her dream of a design studio, and the arm reaching to Earth represented dealing with a very clear and present reality. Dreams and reality merged when both arms returned to center, yet the most essential element was the stretch—upward to dreams and downward to reality. The stretch itself lengthened and strengthened Melinda's long spine and made *her* feel strong and empowered.

I could easily identify with the feelings Melinda had been having. Back in my fast-track days, when I was a young up-and-comer on Madison Avenue, I, too, was dancing someone else's steps. The vague discontent that haunted me was rooted in the simple truth that I was following a script I hadn't actually written. Of course, no one could have convinced me of that notion, because at some point during my undergraduate years, I'd latched onto the idea that getting an MBA would be "cool," going into business would make me a standout, and succeeding in advertising would be "different." I got the MBA, went into business, succeeded in advertising, and am pleased to say that I did it all well, but there was one big problem: The whole show was being choreographed by some tenuous notion about what would impress people. This was someone else's path through life, not mine.

I realized it the night I went to my first Tai Ji class and did the Sky and Earth movement. I reached up to sky and touched the spiritual, and I reached down to Earth and was grounded in reality. Inside me, it felt like coming home after being away my whole life. *The life I'm living isn't mine*, I remember thinking, as I made contact for the first time with the core of my self. *It's not my path, and it's not my purpose.*

For me, the revelation was instantaneous and overwhelming. It was almost as dramatic for Melinda. She decided to end her partnership with Tom and Janice, which

was a bold move, full of backbone. The consequences? Melinda left Tom and Janice to their business plan and in short order opened her own design studio as sole proprietor. She was soon swamped with business and had to hire another designer, then another. At last count, there were four designers working full time with Melinda. Meanwhile, the business Tom and Janice started went belly-up without Melinda's talent and expertise.

More important to Melinda is the fact that she now knows how to stand up for herself and her beliefs—straight and strong.

Intend

- *I intend to feel empowered and confident in myself.*

Affirm

- *I am strong, centered, and grounded.*

Move

- *Sky and Earth*

Judy Garland said it well: "Always be a first-rate version of yourself, rather than a second-rate version of somebody else." Let movement open the real you, stretch your potential, and help you "remember" your authentic self. Then dance your own dance—even in public!

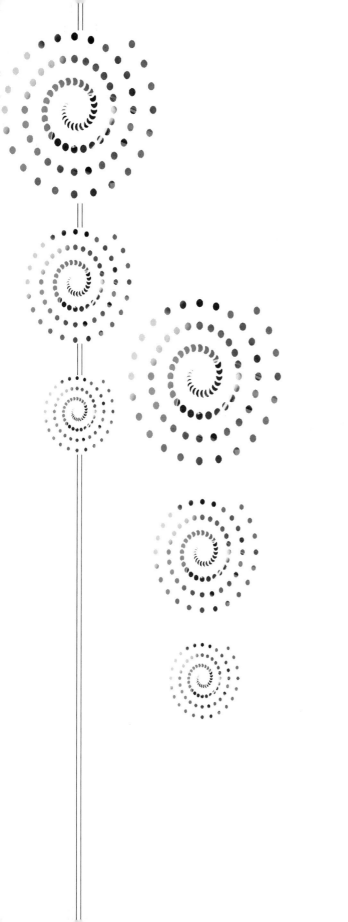

Chapter Seven

Midlife Course Corrections: Finding and Following Your Life's Passion

"Follow your bliss."

— Joseph Campbell

*A*re you following your bliss? Are you pursuing the particular happiness that speaks to your very essence—to the most "you" part of you? If not, then it's time to change the course of your life. It's time to find and follow your passion, to aim your life in the direction of your bliss.

The first step to following your bliss is to get clear about what it is; that is, you have to find your passion before you can follow it. And it must be *your* passion—not someone else's idea of what you should do with your life, what you'd be good at, or what you'd enjoy. Since your parents, friends, teachers, or mentors can't see inside you, they shouldn't be able to decide who you really are and how you really want to live.

It's at your core that you'll find your passion. The Chinese call that core *pu,* a word that translates to "your original face," the face you wore before the mask was put on. There are three Moving Affirmations that will help get you back to *pu,* hone down to the nugget of essential *you*ness, and polish that nugget until it shines brilliantly. They're the Fire, Gold, and Wood movements; shift your movements through them, and you can find your bliss, open yourself to it, trust it, and follow it.

Maybe your bliss lies in a career choice that you put aside for "practical" reasons, a hobby you promised yourself you'd get back to one day, or something creative within you that needs to be expressed. It's possible that you've had a revelation of a way to live or a path to follow—as I did when I was 25—and you've found that your life is at a turning point, as the dreams you dreamed at one stage yield to a new set of values and wishes.

Whatever the source of your bliss, bear in mind that your age doesn't matter; it's neither too late nor too early to make a midcourse correction and change the compass setting of your life. Otherwise, the question your life will be: *What am I willing to settle for?*

When Howard came to see me, he had the sense that he was doing a lot of "settling." He felt a vague dissatisfaction with his work, but he couldn't pin it down or articulate it. At 45, he was a vice president of a Fortune 500 company located in New York City—a position many people would envy. He was appreciated and well paid, and he was even allowed six weeks of vacation a year. But his dissatisfaction (nebulous though it was) continued to eat at him, so Howard and I began to work together.

The Fire movement vividly demonstrated Howard's listlessness. Actually, the only thing vivid about it was his *lack* of vitality; the fire in his movement looked like it would never catch. His motions were unfocused and undirected, with nothing motivating them. It was as if he was trying to ignite a spark with wet wood; and the result was insipid, feeble, and insubstantial. So I tried to get Howard to talk about what really excited him. Sheepishly,

he admitted that when he was younger he'd wanted to be an actor. His family had talked him out of it, insisting it was a totally impractical way to make a living. But Howard was still an avid theatergoer, and the more we focused on adding the element of fire to his movements, the more he thought about and talked about acting. Yet despite his obvious passion, he completely pooh-poohed the suggestion that he might still become an actor.

As he continued to practice the Fire movement, though, the idea grew on him. He realized that he'd already made enough money to live on—even if it meant adopting a more modest lifestyle. So when his next vacation rolled around, he took the six weeks to work in summer stock and again caught the acting bug—badly. This time, Howard decided to quit his job. Against the advice of well-meaning friends and family, who told him he was crazy, Howard and a colleague formed a small theater company of their own, eventually turning it into a viable and successful venture. They're currently building a new off-Broadway theater in New York, and they've scheduled a complete season of productions for the coming year.

Some people think Howard is less successful now than when he was a "suit" in the corporate world, and to be sure, he's making far less money. But in his own eyes, he's far more successful. He's *living* his life now—and loving it. He's following his bliss.

See It, Then Go for It

> *"The real voyage of discovery consists not in seeking*
> *new landscapes, but in having new eyes."*
> — Marcel Proust

Just as the Fire movement ignites your buried passion, the Wood movement gives you new eyes and opens you to new possibilities. Consider the metaphorical basis of the movement. A tree has no front and no rear; rather, it's open to all possibilities from any direction—the full 360 degrees. That's essential, because sometimes before you can identify your bliss, you have to see what's out there. Once you do, you're ready to bring into yourself just what's needed to equip you for that new voyage of discovery.

Like Howard, Deborah seemed to have it all. Among the things she had were good looks, health, wealth, a loving husband, and a palatial apartment overlooking New York's Central Park. By any external measure, Deborah's life looked secure and happy. Yet every morning, as she rifled through the extensive wardrobe in her spacious closet to pick out something to wear that day, she found the prospect of her life unexciting, unfulfilling, and dim.

For reasons even Deborah couldn't articulate, she began to work with me. Something must have been telling her that this "secure and happy" life wasn't for her, because on my regular trips to New York to see students, she'd invariably book sessions with me. For two full years, she'd phone monthly to arrange sessions with me each time I was in New York, but once I'd return to California, she'd fail to keep up the practice, or work on any of the movements on her own. She was only inching toward change.

I didn't push her, for Deborah's body language showed me that she wasn't yet prepared for change. For example, where the Wood movement called for her to extend her arms out and pivot a full 360 degrees, she simply walked around a square of the floor, her arms slack at her sides. Similarly, when asked to reach in the Gold movement, Deborah's arm stretched out, but her eyes didn't follow and her hips didn't open. The message? I could see that while she wanted to reach for something else, she really wasn't ready to see the potential "something elses" out there.

All of this was understandable. Change isn't easy, and it often takes time to work up to it. People need to honor their own timing, and I wasn't about to press the point with Deborah. But finally, after two years of our sessions together, the time was suddenly right. In the Wood movement, Deborah's arms spread out like the branches of a tree, and both her body and her vision turned a full 360 degrees, taking in all perspectives. In the Gold movement, as she reached out for the possibilities, her body finally opened fully, ready to receive what she needed and go after what was right for her. It had taken years for Deborah to develop the inner strength she needed to be ready; once she began to shift her movements, however, her life transformation was swift and radical.

It turns out that the hustle and bustle of the glamorous Fifth Avenue life was very far from what Deborah craved. Although she really tried to make it work with her husband, they discovered that they wanted vastly different things from life. So Deborah left New York, and she left her marriage. She went to the other side of the continent—both literally and in terms of lifestyle—moving to Oregon and learning to be a healer. Having seen 360 degrees' worth of possibilities, Deborah made a 180-degree change in her life. She now leads a simple life with very little money, but it has made her extraordinarily happy.

If you can't see the new landscape of your life's transformation, then maybe you need a fresh set of eyes. Try the movements as Deborah did:

Intend

- *I intend to be open to life's possibilities.*

Affirm

- *I can succeed at anything I choose.*

Move

- *Wood*

Too Late?

There's no such thing as being too old, too set in your ways, or too married to a person, job, or way of life to reach for the kind of happiness Deborah attained. The great writer George Eliot put it well in a wonderful phrase: "It is never too late to be what you might have been."

A client of mine named Lynn really proved the validity of this statement. She'd wanted to be an architect when she was a young woman, but her father nixed the idea. In that era, and in a Southern family that prized the traditions of an earlier century, patriarchal disapproval wasn't easily dismissed. Lynn made some tentative efforts at defiance, but they didn't work. And years later, she'd learn that her father had gone to some lengths to thwart her dream: He'd actually sifted through her college applications and dumped the ones to schools with important architecture departments. He wanted his daughter to be a good wife and mother, and he was willing to do all he could to make sure that's what she became.

Lynn did become a good wife and mother—and a happy one. She was a fixture in the local community, always lending a helping hand to charities and school events. When she came to my studio for "stretching exercises," as she put it, she did them as dutifully as you might expect of a nice Southern belle. She copied my movements exactly—but dispassionately. There was no life or vitality in her movements; she was simply going through the motions.

Of course, as we began to explore the reason for her lackluster execution of the Moving Affirmations, it became clear that she was just "going through the motions" in her life as well. Her existence was a carbon copy of a magazine article written by someone else, just as her movements in the studio were cookie-cutter replicas of my movements.

The more we worked together, the more involved Lynn became in the study of Tai Ji. She was very intrigued by Chinese culture—in particular, its art and architecture—and it became clear that Lynn's youthful dream to be an architect had never died. With the support of her husband and son, Lynn took the exams for architecture school, was accepted, and moved (with her entire family) to the state where the university was located. She did her graduate work, and today she's a licensed architect working hard at a profession she absolutely loves.

Lynn hadn't been an unhappy woman before, but she'd been a woman who still ached for an old dream. Going for it has transformed her life and has given her the fulfillment that was missing. Where following your bliss is concerned, it's truly never too late.

If you're someone who has worried that life has passed you by, it hasn't. You still have time to go for it, as Lynn did:

 Intend

- *I intend to become [fill in the blank].*

 Affirm

- *I deserve to be and do what I want. I can succeed.
  I am in charge of my destiny.*

Move

- *Gold*

"Think Mystery, Not Mastery"

Julia Cameron, bestselling author on the subject of creativity, wrote: "Do what intrigues you, explore what interests you: Think mystery, not mastery." It's an ongoing concept, and it applies perfectly to my student Rae.

Rae held one of those fabled "high-powered" jobs in the movie industry. She hobnobbed with stars, traveled first class, and had a phalanx of assistants and aides constantly ready to execute her every command. She enjoyed her work, and she was very, very good at it.

Increasingly, however, there were times when Rae found the pace overwhelming and wished she could have some time to think. And there were days and nights when she wished that there were someone she could share her life with—a sympathetic and supportive partner who'd provide the perfect happy ending to her own personal movie.

Of course, the way things were going, Rae had no time to form a relationship—even though she met many fascinating men. And although she couldn't imagine *not* working, she frequently felt oppressed by the pressures of corporate life. So when she came to see me, it was out of a desire to be open to change—maybe to a new kind of work, and perhaps to a new and lasting relationship.

Watching Rae perform the Wood movement, I could see that she looked seriously unhappy as she surveyed what was around her. When it was time to let go, she hesitated and then tried to control the movement. It was clear to me that what she saw in her existing field of vision wasn't enough for her anymore.

The first step was to open up Rae's vision, so we focused on clearing her mind and looking beyond the immediate in the Wood movement. We created specific intentions, affirmations, and visualizations to do this. Then we turned to the Gold movement and extended her arm's reach and her body's openness, inviting in what was right for her.

Within six months, Rae had said farewell—without regret—to her star-studded job, and began training as a psychologist. She met, and has since married, a wonderful man. Together they moved to a new state, bought a gem of a house, and have begun a bright new life together. It was simple: Rae found that the glittering world she'd been living in was no longer for her, so she opened the door, stepped outside, and went for the real gold inside herself.

The point is this: When you go for the gold in the Olympics of your life, your only competition is yourself. All you have to do is try, and you can't lose.

 ### Intend

- *I intend to develop a new life that will be perfect for who I am.*

 ### Affirm

- *I will find the work that is perfect for me now.*

 ### Move

- *Wood*

Intend

- *I intend to bring in a partner who can support who I am and share my life.*

Affirm

- *I deserve a committed, wonderful romantic relationship, and I am open to it now.*

Move

- *Gold*

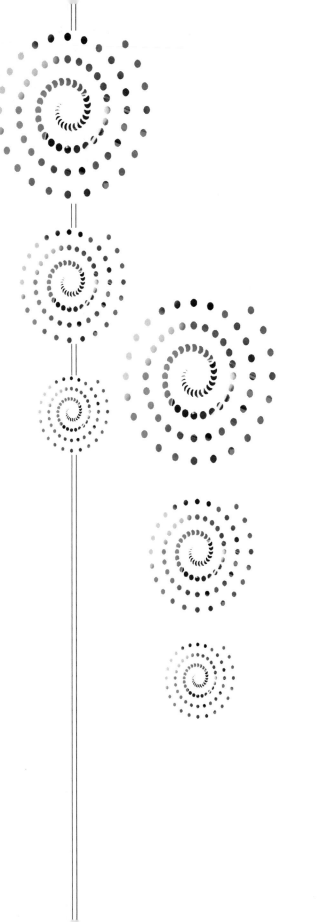

Chapter Eight

Handling Fear, Anxiety, and Stress

"Courage is action in the presence of fear."

— Stewart Emery

There's no such thing as life without fear, anxiety, or stress. There never has been, and there never will be. After all, fear is an important protective measure—your ancestors survived by acting out of fear when pursued by predators, just as anxiety spurred them on to forage for food for their families. Stress furthered the survival of the species, and the result was that fear and anxiety became programmed into the human genetic code.

The ancient Chinese spoke of the "ten thousand things" that clog our lives and wear us down; today, the number must be ten billion. Chances are you don't need to keep one eye open to watch for man-eating beasts, but you probably do experience stress over college tuition bills, performance at work, traffic jams, or crashing computers. Daily worries, cares, concerns, and apprehensions can lodge themselves in your body, and over time, holding on to them can cause physical symptoms. In fact, *stress* is actually a clinical description for increased heart rate, a rise in blood pressure, muscular tension, irritability, and depression. Stress can also cause breathing problems, ulcers, and neck pain—the bodily manifestations of mental and emotional disruptions, the physical results of storing up your cares and concerns tightly within you.

We all have fears, and we often worry for good reason: The future is uncertain. You can't completely rid your life of apprehension and anxiety, and it would be foolish to suppose you could. After all, there's no shortage of scary situations in the world—from random terrorist attacks to lunatic drivers on highways. There's also no end to circumstances that have the potential to produce anxiety or stress, such as being diagnosed with an illness, preparing to make a big presentation at work, or ending a relationship. But you shouldn't shut down your life in the face of challenging situations; instead, you must learn to work with your feelings so that they don't control your life.

Living in fear can immobilize you and make your life numb, but changing the way you move can help; it can break the logjam of fear and lower its intensity, so that you coexist gracefully with whatever frightens you.

Three of the Moving Affirmations in particular are geared to help you deal with your apprehensions and stress. Practicing Gold and Water will restore a sense of safety and give you a calm respite, and Embrace Tiger will remind you that you have the power to go forward fearlessly and face whatever life has to offer.

Coexisting with Reality

Helena was one of my first students, and she also became a good friend. She lived in a small but comfortable rental apartment, with a part-time job as a bookkeeper that allowed her just enough money to support her simple life. So no one was more surprised than she was when the events of September 11, 2001, threw her for a loop. Suddenly, she couldn't sleep. She'd lie awake at night, worrying about the state of the world and her family. She wouldn't get on an airplane, and she avoided crowds. In short, she felt paralyzed.

Helena tried doing the sequence of Moving Affirmations but found that she couldn't remember them all—specifically, she couldn't remember the Wood movement. To me, that was very telling, for the Wood movement (which represents stability and flexibility) shows how confident we are out in the world. Clearly, Helena wasn't confident—she was afraid. And by operating out of fear, she was becoming what she feared being—a victim, a target.

The first step for Helena was to find out where she felt the panic in her body. It was right in her gut—in her tantien center. I asked Helena to focus on her center, noticing her feelings and acknowledging them nonjudgmentally. Then I suggested that she do the Gold movement, reaching out for support with each arm—whatever she needed to feel safe, secure, calm, and at peace.

 ## Intend

- *I intend to have peace and serenity in my life.*

 ## Affirm

- *I feel peaceful and serene.*

 ## Move

- *Gold*

When you're afraid, do the Gold movement several times until your breathing has slowed and stabilized. Stay balanced, with your hands on your tantien center. Remember that you can't change reality—for example, September 11 *did* happen—but you can coexist with it. Start by acknowledging your fear, then release it. Focus on what you want, not on what you're afraid of, and be open to the support you need. Then let go with your hands and your mind, and say aloud: "I release what holds me back from feeling calm."

Dealing with Stress

There aren't many professions more stressful than that of medical doctor. Life and death are in a physician's hands every day. One false move, one misdiagnosis, and the consequences can be absolutely earth-shattering to the patient. Dennis, a surgeon, was acutely aware of those possible consequences, and as a result, stress was his constant companion. He came to me to see if I could help him alleviate his anxiety.

The Water movement is a great antidote to stress, yet Dennis was so tense when he first began his sessions that when I asked him to do the movement, his shoulders remained rigid at the top of his body. So I asked him if there was a waterfall he'd been to that he particularly remembered, and he told me that he'd been to a beautiful one in Hawaii, which was his favorite vacation spot.

"Put yourself there," I suggested. "Imagine yourself standing under that waterfall. Now do the Water movement."

Dennis did the movement; his shoulders instantly released and his face lit up with a smile. After doing it four more times, Dennis was completely relaxed in both body and mind.

I suggest that you do the same: Put yourself under your favorite waterfall—a lush, secluded place, with green moss and cool blue water. Now do the Water movement. Flow with the waterfall—and take a break from the stress you can't avoid.

 Intend

- *I intend to radiate peace and calm as I move through my life.*

 Affirm

- *I feel relaxed.*

 Move

- *Water*

Embrace Your Tiger

There's a Chinese folktale about a farmer whose horse ran away. "Oh, bad luck," said the farmer's neighbors, "don't you think?"

"Perhaps," the farmer replied. The next day, however, his horse came back—bringing with him ten valuable wild stallions.

"Oh, you have good luck!" the neighbors exclaimed.

"Perhaps," said the farmer.

The next day, the farmer's son went to ride one of the new stallions. He was thrown from the horse and broke a leg.

There were the neighbors again: "Bad luck," they said, "don't you think?"

The farmer replied as usual: "Perhaps."

The next day, government agents went door-to-door to draft all the young men for a border war. But when they saw the farmer's son in bed with a broken leg, they said, "Keep your son, farmer; he's no good to us!"

The neighbors showed up, declaring: "Now finally you must admit that this is good luck!"

You can guess the farmer's reply: "Perhaps."

The point is that we don't really know what's good and what's bad. Something that seems like a blessing might turn out to be a burden, and vice versa—and it's rare that something is wholly one or the other. Only in retrospect can we affirm what worked and what was right for us. But once we've learned to handle the fears, anxiety, and stressful situations that are an integral part of life, we're ready to go out and catch whatever wave life is sending us. That's what the Embrace Tiger movement is all about.

For many years, I've shared my Moving Affirmations with HIV and AIDS patients. One particular group, from The Mind/Body Medical Institute in Massachusetts, has some of the longest-living survivors of the disease. They discuss the *gifts* that having this disease has brought into their lives, and with rare exceptions, they say that the quality of their lives and the depth of their relationships with others has actually changed for the better since their diagnosis. Would they wish HIV or AIDS on others? No, of course not. But they embrace what their experience has given them, and they *use* it. Certainly, they've all gone through denial, resentment, anger, and sadness, but in time they've found the blessing in the curse.

Embrace Tiger reminds us to do just that. It asks us to enjoy what is wondrous, and it teaches us to accept the "bad" in life and deal with it with grace, dignity, and even joy. Imagine yourself going out to embrace a real tiger—a beautiful, dangerous animal. Then think about embracing the tiger within you—an audacious, graceful, extraordinary creature, eager and unafraid to go after life and all it has to offer.

Once you've dealt with your fears and anxiety and you know how to find respite from stress, you're ready to Embrace Tiger even when the Tiger is at its fiercest and most destructive. For example, when Alice first came to me, she was facing one of the worst health problems you can imagine—a brain tumor. Understandably, she was frightened. But Alice's fear was so intense that she was unable to make any decisions about her health. She simply didn't want to face the issue. What's more, she *knew* she didn't want to face the issue; that's why she came to me.

Right away I noticed that Alice routinely forgot Embrace Tiger when we went through the sequence of Moving Affirmations. She wasn't dealing with her illness, and she certainly wasn't embracing it.

Intellectually, Alice was aware that she had to act. She knew that she had to learn all there was to know about her tumor, consider treatment options, and make decisions. She just couldn't bring herself to do it. She was emotionally—and physically—incapable of dealing with this most serious challenge.

I suggested that Alice reconnect with the sky and the earth so that she'd feel safe enough to deal with her life at the moment. We worked on Embrace Tiger, and she made the connection that both grounded her and opened her to the spiritual. She was now ready to receive information from the medical community and to ask for help from her friends.

In time, Alice found the right doctor and medical treatment. Today, more than a decade since her tumor was diagnosed, she's in remission and living a full and healthy life.

As you do the movement, open one arm to the sky, with your fingers pointed upward, and bring your other arm to earth. Feel a sense of openness in your heart and center, and think about getting support from both sides—the spiritual and the earthbound. Then bring both hands together at your tantien center, where these forces meet and merge. Hold your hands at your center and think about being open to receiving support, guidance, and strength. Think about the challenge you face—whether it's an illness or a career change, a decision about marriage or a job interview—and cross your arms and hands in front of you as if embracing a loving, compassionate being. Say: "I choose to feel strong, and I accept the challenges and the gifts that this situation brings me."

Now embrace the tiger within—and go out and grab life by the tail.

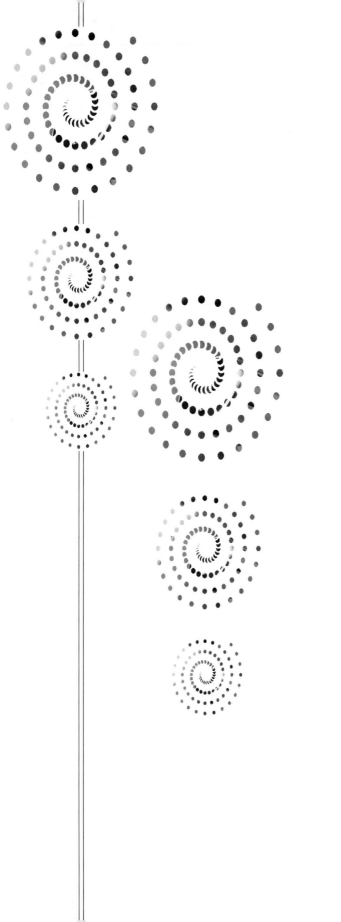

Chapter Nine

Liberating Body and Mind: Letting Go of Unhealthy Habits

"If a man is at any time to have a chance of escape,

then he must first of all realize that he is in prison."

— G. I. Gurdjieff

We live by habits—acquired patterns of behavior so automatic that we're not even conscious of them. Consider the way you prepare and drink your morning coffee or tea, or your daily ritual of undressing, brushing your teeth, and preparing for bed. And let's not forget about work habits: I have a friend who might be unrecognizable without a pencil behind her ear and her glasses hiked up on her forehead, and there's a certain business executive I know who always reads reports with a yellow highlighter in his hand—and even when he's reading something on his computer screen, he still needs to hold a highlighter.

Habits are learned behavior. Renowned educator Horace Mann once wrote: "Habit is a cable; we weave a thread of it each day, and at last we cannot break it." For example, I remember when the seat-belt law was passed in my state. At first, it was annoying and inconvenient to force myself to buckle up every time I wanted to drive to the store for a newspaper or a quart of milk. Now, of course, it's automatic and essential; I feel naked without my seat belt on, and wouldn't think of driving unless I were strapped in.

Like buckling up when in a car, many habits are benign, even beneficial. Some qualify as quirks—my friend's pencil behind the ear, for example, looks especially strange in this era of Palm Pilots. But some habits are fundamentally destructive—such as alcoholism, compulsive cleaning, nail-biting, obsessive Web-surfing, even the habit of going from one unsupportive lover to the next. While none of these habits may kill you, any and all can wreak havoc on your self-esteem, deplete your bank account, ruin your appearance, burden a friendship, poison a love affair, and make you very unhappy. Instead of being master of your fate, you're held prisoner by your habit, and that's not healthy at all.

Destructive habitual behavior is never really about the behavior; it's about the underlying *cause* of the behavior. Invariably, it's a symptom of something lacking in your life, a way of masking feelings of emptiness, and an attempt to fill a void. Unfortunately, because the habit is repeated unconsciously, there's no connection between the behavior and the fact that it doesn't work. All you do is dull the pain momentarily without dealing with the root cause, so you'll soon need to repeat the action again and again and again—probably at a higher "dose." The deep wound continues to fester, and the pain becomes even more acute.

I see this dynamic at work when students with destructive habitual behavior do the Sky and Earth movement. Where the movement calls for them to bring sky and earth together at the tantien center by rolling hand over hand, these students get stuck—they loop their hands over and over and over. This action continues until I tell them to stop.

It's a reflection of how they feel in their lives: No matter what they do, they can't get enough. They never feel satisfied, so they keep on trying to fill up the hole.

Before we go any further, let me be perfectly clear about one thing: No form of movement practice on its own can heal a true addiction. Dependence on alcohol, nicotine, or drugs are complex syndromes that require expert medical attention. This book makes no claim whatsoever to deal with such problems. If you're addicted to smoking, alcohol, and/or controlled substances, I advise you to seek appropriate medical advice and therapy. Moving Affirmations can help support your recovery process, but they're by no means a substitute for the right treatment administered by those individuals and organizations specializing in addiction recovery.

Even if your destructive habit isn't controlled-substance related, this movement practice may not solve your problem on its own. Changing your behavior is a task that only you can do, but specialists can help guide you to the most effective ways to accomplish your goals. In fact, the Moving Affirmations work particularly well when you do them in conjunction with other forms of therapy. The movements sharpen your insight into what's causing your particular behavior and why; and they provide balance, relaxation, relief from stress, and the kind of spiritual nourishment that dramatically advances the healing process.

Recognize Your Prison

What's the behavior you want to liberate yourself from? Do you shop compulsively, spending money hand over fist whenever you feel a little low? Do you overeat—then hate yourself for it? Do you spend hours and hours chatting with strangers on the Internet, in turn isolating yourself from your family and friends? I'll bet it shows when you do the Sky and Earth movement, manifesting as an imbalance when you go to join sky and earth. Chinese philosophers believe that it's this point of convergence and connection—the movement joining Sky and Earth—that leads to a state of oneness with the cosmos, affirming the unity of yin and yang, male and female, mother and father, and all our opposite aspects. Thus, being off balance confirms a very fundamental conflict.

So what's lacking in your life that makes you unable to connect sky and earth? Answer that, and you'll know the underlying cause of your destructive habitual behavior. Know the cause, and you can begin the healing.

Bringing in What You Need

Liz came to see me many years ago, bringing with her a host of health problems. She had heart palpitations, soreness in her leg muscles, and poor circulation. Yet all of these were mere side effects of a bigger problem, the reason she'd come to see me in the first place—her weight.

Clinically, Liz would have been classified as "morbidly obese." She weighed 120 pounds more than the acceptable weight for her size and age. It wasn't that she couldn't lose weight; Liz had been "on every diet in the world," in her words, and had yo-yoed all over the place. It wasn't unusual for her to lose up to 100 pounds on a diet, only to gain it all back, plus another 20. By her own estimation, she'd lost and gained more than 1,000 pounds over the years on her dieting roller coaster. She was now heavier than ever, miserable, and searching for a way to stop the swinging pendulum of starvation and overeating.

When I asked Liz to perform the Sky and Earth movement, she would gather both elements, then bring her hands together into fists, as if holding on for dear life. And she'd continually roll her hands in circles toward her center. Remember that the movement calls for one loop with the hands—a single turn. But Liz couldn't stop; she kept rolling her fists over and over and over again, as if she could never get enough and she had to keep on grabbing and holding on as tightly as possible. Liz's movements showed that emotionally, she was neither savoring the moment nor taking in only what was right for her; on the contrary, she was trying to grasp for too much and hold on to everything. Her overeating was a perfect metaphor for her life: Liz shoveled food down without tasting it, and she was scared to let go of it, lest she feel empty.

I pointed this out to her, and we began to talk. "What is it," I asked Liz, "that you're trying to bring in and hold on to so tenaciously?" The question brought tears to her eyes, and it prompted memories of a childhood in which she'd received many material comforts but almost no attention from her family. Neither parent gave her the love she craved, but above all, she felt profound regret at having missed the love of her father—an imposing and successful man whom she'd adored. She'd always sought his affection and support, but they were never forthcoming.

Naturally, Liz's failure to receive the love she'd wanted had left her with a deep sense of scarcity, which was the underlying cause of the destructive overeating that plagued her. She turned to food to fill a void, but since it wasn't food that she really wanted or needed, she was never satisfied; no matter how much food she took in, it could never be enough.

Both of Liz's parents were now dead, so she couldn't go back and try to establish a better relationship with them. Instead, we focused on her eagerness to find a spiritual dimension in her life, which was a reflection of the fatherly love she desired. (As I stated in Chapter 2, the Chinese philosophy of yin and yang asserts that yang principles are

assertive and male—sun, creation, heat, light, and heaven; yin principles are receptive and female—moon, cold, darkness, submission, and earth.) By forging the spiritual connection Liz sought, I hoped that we'd lessen her sense of scarcity.

In order to make that spiritual connection, Liz and I practiced changing the way she moved. Liz's multiple loops in Sky and Earth had been excessively rushed, and her tight fists told a story of frantic grasping, so step one was to slow the movement, reduce it to a single loop, and open her hands so that she was taking in only what was right for her.

I asked Liz to hold one hand up to the sky, fingers open, and the other hand down toward the earth. "Now," I instructed, "slowly, with open hands, blend sky and earth one time only, in a single loop." Liz began to do the movement at a slow-motion pace. "Feel it," I told her. "Savor it. Slow it down and really take it in."

We did the movement for several minutes. When we finished, Liz was back in balance. Her face, which had looked so worried when she first walked into the studio, now wore an expression of pure peace and contentment. She was aware that she'd sought nourishment in all the wrong places, and that was a crucial step. I asked Liz to focus on doing the Sky and Earth movement at that same slow pace every day for the next several weeks. To bring home the point, she created an intention of feeling supported and nourished, as well as an affirmation, done with an open hand, that she was bringing in exactly what she needed. To experience the fullness you desire, try Liz's Moving Affirmation:

Intend

- *I intend to be supported, loved, and nourished.*
- *I intend to lose my unhealthy excess weight and to resolve my underlying issues.*

Affirm

- *I bring in exactly what I need at this moment.*
- *I feel abundant; I feel fully nourished.*

Move

- *Sky and Earth*

Each time Liz did the movement, it reminded her to slow down her intake and let go when she'd had enough. Scarcity turned into sufficiency, strengthening her sense of self.

Greater confidence made it possible for her to bring in friends as a support system, and the encouragement she received from them reinforced her ability to make peace with te fact that she'd never received the parental love she'd craved.

Over time, as Liz concentrated on practicing the movement, a shift began to take place. As she focused on feeling the connection to sky and earth and thought about inviting both fully into her center, she began to change. She understood intellectually that she'd filled up on food as a substitute for something else and that it hadn't worked. That awareness allowed her to approach eating more mindfully—to savor food, not stuff it in. She went on a daily walk and practiced meditation every morning, and she began to lose weight for a very simple reason: She was beginning to feel spiritually and emotionally nourished.

Getting Rid of What No Longer Serves You

Even as you bring in what you need for nourishment, you must also release what no longer serves you. Liz needed to lighten her load, both physically and psychologically. Her excess weight had served as a buffer, a defense mechanism against getting close to others or becoming involved in intimate relationships. For a woman who'd never received the love she needed, such intimacy could be frightening, even if it was what she really wanted.

To help Liz let go, we worked out a set of intentions, affirmations, and visualizations that emphasized freedom from excess weight. I added the Flight of the Eagle Moving Affirmation to Liz's regime to help her free her bodymind, and I asked her to focus on keeping her hands open while doing it.

 Intend

- *I intend to let my body find its natural and healthy weight.*

 Affirm

- *I release what I no longer need.*
- *I feel free.*

 M o v e

- *Flight of the Eagle*

It took months of daily affirmations for Liz to effect the transformation she sought, but it did happen. She lost the weight she wanted to lose; she became the "slim Liz" she'd visualized while doing Sky and Earth.

That was many years ago. Liz maintains a healthy weight to this day, and the reason is simple: She's able to bring all the nourishment she needs into her center, and can let go of whatever no longer serves her. She's free of the habitual behavior that was destroying her—as free as a bird in flight.

Having Enough, Being Enough

Hannah came to me wanting to work through a case of what she wryly called "retail therapy." At the slightest upset, she'd go shopping for a dress, a cashmere sweater, a new food processor, or a high-tech telephone with caller ID. As she handed over her credit card and watched each purchase being packaged, she felt a rush of excitement, a momentary absence of pain. But of course, the feeling was fleeting. By the time Hannah pulled into her driveway and began to haul her purchases into the house, the thrill was gone. What remained was depression, anger, emptiness, and yet another dip into the household bank account.

So Hannah bought more. Even though it put her in debt, she bought generously; giving extravagant gifts produced a different kind of thrill, even though it was equally transient. The first time I met her, at a weekend workshop I was running, she drove to a nearby town and bought out its gourmet shop, providing French cheeses, Greek olives, Italian sausages, and all sorts of mustards, honeys, olive oils, and vinegars to each of the 20 people attending the session. It was generous, but excessively so—and it embarrassed the other workshop attendees, who saw the action for what it really was: a clear statement of a destructive form of habitual behavior.

When I had Hannah do the Sky and Earth movement, she grabbed and pulled into center, and her arms turned over and over and over like endlessly flapping wings. Her movements, like Liz's, reflected her attempt to get all she could, to fill up, and to hold on. Clearly, her buying sprees were temporary fixes for a long-term problem, yet she was caught in the viselike grip of her shopping habit.

Where was the emptiness in Hannah's life? It took a while to determine. She told me that she was married to a wonderful man who constantly demonstrated his love for her, she was the mother of two wonderful children, and she had friends galore. I soon began to wonder why, if everything was so perfect, Hannah was in my studio asking for help.

Of course, the story behind the story eventually came out. The loving husband was a workaholic who was rarely around. He traveled frequently and stayed in the office until midnight even when he was in town, and his demonstrations of love came in the form of gifts intended to stave off Hannah's complaints about his absence. The wonderful children were away at college and rarely contacted their mother. On school vacations, they'd drop by to see Mom and Dad and then head off to hang out with their buddies. As for Hannah's friends, they were indeed numerous. The problem was that they all had careers, and when the workday was over, they went home to their families. Hannah felt alone, bored, useless, and unloved; shopping filled the time, but it didn't fill the black hole of her feelings.

Awareness would have to be the first step. Hannah needed to acknowledge that the emptiness in her life couldn't be filled with yet another handbag, and a bottle of perfume couldn't assuage her anguish nor eliminate its root. To achieve that awareness, we started slowly, spinning out the motions of the Sky and Earth movement so that Hannah could take the time to reflect on what she really needed. Here is Hannah's Sky and Earth routine:

 Intend

- *I intend to learn to deal with my problems, not escape them.*

Affirm

- *I feel supported and connected to the earth and to a higher power.*
- *I accept myself as I am.*

 Move

- *Sky and Earth*

At the same time she was doing the Moving Affirmations, Hannah was also working with her psychotherapist. This provided a "double whammy" effect: The movement practice enhanced the work with the therapist, and the work with the therapist articulated an intellectual basis for the work Hannah was doing with me. It allowed her to analyze the underlying causes of her feelings of emptiness—to understand the void in her life and to gain insight into why her "solution" had taken the form of shopping for things.

Then we added the Flight of the Eagle to her movement practice. Her focus on Sky and Earth gave her a better sense of who she was and let her feel that she was enough; now she needed to fly through the bars of her prison and release the shopping habit.

Here's how Hannah soared:

Intend

- *I intend to free myself of all addictive and unsupportive behaviors.*

Affirm

- *I release all that holds me back from being the best I can be.*

Move

- *Flight of the Eagle*

"To fall into a habit is to begin to cease to be," wrote Spanish author and philosopher Miguel de Unamuno. Any habit can be a prison, but destructive habits can be a life sentence. Shift your movements, and you can begin to identify the lack in your life, bring in nourishment that fills you, let go of destructive habits, break free, and soar on the wings of an eagle.

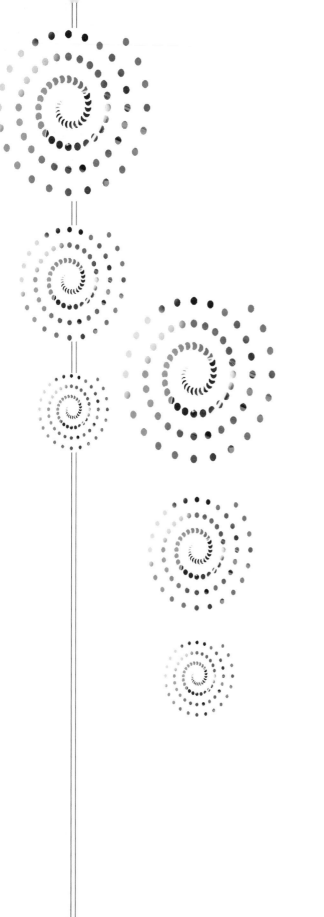

Chapter Ten
Getting a Relationship

"The subject of relationship must begin with you."

— Emmanuel

Relationships aren't easy.

They can cause tension and require compromise, and they often end—having failed to meet the needs of one or both partners. Yet we crave them, which is entirely natural. In fact, there's more than a little evidence suggesting that intimacy between two people is an inherent necessity of the human condition.

Way back in our prehistoric past, we humans found ourselves relatively defenseless. For all our dexterity and ingenuity, we lacked the natural defenses that many animals are equipped with—we didn't have as keen a sense of smell, the ability to camouflage ourselves, remarkable speed, or fierce claws. To survive, we had to band together. Our relationships made the survival and propagation of our species possible, and eventually ensured human dominion over nature. So if you've ever wondered why you keep craving a relationship—despite the fact that every one you've had has failed—be aware that desiring a partnership with another person is programmed into your genetic code.

But what does it take to form a union with someone? The first requirement is that you're open to *all* that a relationship can bring: pain and joy, difficulty and comfort. Woody Allen once said that "eighty percent of success is showing up." Well, that means you're going to have to be willing to love and be loved, to care and be cared for. If you want a loving relationship but you've never had one; or never had one that really worked; or had one, lost it, and continue to look for that just-right match again, you must begin by healing your relationship with *yourself*.

Of course, that's why you're reading this book—to become the person you want to be, the person you know you really are inside, so that you can live the life you desire. And now you're ready to turn up the volume and look at the specific barriers that may be keeping you from entering into a relationship with another person. Some of these obstacles may have been put in your path by circumstance; some of them you may have constructed yourself. Whatever your situation, three Moving Affirmations will help you demolish the roadblocks; they'll open the way for you to have a relationship with a person who's right for you. They are: Step Out of the Box, Open Your Heart and Mind; Golden Lotus; and Wood.

What Your Movements Are Saying

Just about everyone who comes to my studio claims that they want to have a deep, committed relationship—at least that's the message their *words* convey. But when I ask them to do the Step Out of the Box, Open Your Heart and Mind movement, their *bodies* tell a very different story.

Women are generally the ones who overextend when they do the movement, throwing their chests forward and opening their arms way out to the side. It's an awkward and unnatural movement, and it screams out the message: "Take me!" It reveals a kind of desperation that's bound to frighten people away, and it almost always does.

The other extreme occurs when people do just the opposite: They collapse their chests inward, thrust their shoulders forward, and push their hands out and away. "I'm emotionally unavailable; don't come near me," is the signal this posture gives off, and people can see that.

Whether you're exceedingly needy or closed off, it shows—not just in doing the Step Out of the Box, Open Your Heart and Mind Moving Affirmation, but in your attitude, the way you carry yourself, and how you respond to others. Your voice may be articulating one message, but your body is proclaiming something very different, and it's body language that comes through the loudest.

. . ˙ ˙ . . .

Nina came to my studio late one winter afternoon. She really wanted a meaningful bond with a man and couldn't understand why she'd experienced so many disappointments in her relationships. Yet her very first movement—Step Out of the Box, Open Your Heart and Mind—revealed a woman tightly closed off to others. I could see that Nina was someone who kept her emotional distance.

I talked to Nina about being centered and asked her to think about all three of her centers (tantien, heartmind, and third eye), but to focus on the first two—tantien and heartmind. I suggested that she think of herself as being supported by her centers, and as connected through them to both sky and earth. In other words, I wanted Nina to feel grounded and stable. "Know that you are supported," I told her. "Now, let's do the movement again."

Nina stood with her arms crossed, wrists in front of her chest. I instructed her to open her hands at chest level. "Keep your focus soft and don't look too hard." Nina did the movement again. In fact, I asked her to repeat the movement for several minutes—opening, opening, and opening yet again, peeling away the layers that had been placed over her heart through the years.

All of a sudden, tears came to Nina's eyes. "What is it?" I asked. She told me that she'd suddenly flashed back to the moment in her childhood when her father left the house—after which he'd made little attempt to be part of her life. She had only been five at the time, but from that point on, her mother was full of bitterness and resentment. Nina, too, had always taken the loss of her father as a personal affront. As a result, she'd kept men at arm's length, even though she admitted that the distancing had exacted a stiff emotional price. Although part of her was ready for a relationship, Nina acknowledged that she still felt fearful.

I suggested that by shifting her movement to achieve balance in opening her heart and mind, she could transform her love life; she could become receptive to a man without giving off her usual negative vibe. Nina was incredulous: "How can changing my movement shift what's happening in my life? It just sounds silly," she said. But after some persuasion, she agreed that "it couldn't hurt to try."

Again, she stood with her arms crossed at her wrists in front of her chest. Reluctantly, she opened her chest and arms, announcing her intention—"I intend to be willing to let a man who is right for me into my life"—and affirming that she was lovable. She visualized peeling back and lifting off layer after layer that had grown over her heart.

Nina did the Moving Affirmation several times. Then I asked her to do the Golden Lotus movement, with the intention of having a loving, supportive relationship and affirming that she deserved it. In time, Nina came to believe that message, and her intentions began to come true. By spring, just a few months after she'd first come to my studio, Nina met a man she felt she could become close to, and the wound of her father's abandonment began to heal. She continues to do the movements today; they're supporting the change in herself and the transformation in her life.

Undeserving?

So many women who have taken movement sessions with me are convinced that they're "undeserving." Ann felt that way, despite the fact that her looks made her a magnet for men. Time and again, she'd managed to sabotage the relationships she formed—either by attracting men who emotionally abused her or by pushing away those who seemed to get too close.

It turned out that behind her extremely attractive facade, Ann carried inner scars, caused primarily by a father who bullied her and virtually never showed affection. Finding men who repeated that paternal pattern was easy, but it took its toll, and eventually those relationships would end. And when a man didn't treat her in the abusive way her father had, she couldn't quite relate to him, so those relationships would end as well. Ann simply didn't see herself as deserving a supportive, loving, caring mate. When I asked her to devise an affirmation about her own lovability, she couldn't find the words; the idea was too distant from her image of herself.

I knew that I could tell Ann over and over that she deserved a loving relationship with someone who was exactly right for her. (She did, and so do you. In fact, we're all worthy of being cared for.) But Ann needed to believe this herself. She had to accept that she was worthy; otherwise, she'd continue to self-sabotage. After all, when you believe that you're unworthy of being loved, you'll only attract people who support that belief—that is, people who either can't or won't treat you with affection and respect.

But accepting yourself as worthy and deserving may require some healing work. I knew that Ann needed to start small, with a single positive thought she could buy into: "I am beginning to be lovable." Over time, as she did the Golden Lotus and Step Out of the Box,

Open Your Heart and Mind movements with this affirmation, Ann began to feel a bit more confident. Then she shifted her affirmation slightly: "My willingness to accept a supportive and loving relationship is growing." That proved to be even more nourishing, and Ann's positive self-image began to blossom. As it did—and as she began to believe in her own worth—she began to attract the kind of men who supported her new belief.

Try it Ann's way:

Intend

- *I intend to believe in myself as a worthwhile, loving, and lovable person who deserves affection and respect.*

- *I intend to open myself to loving relationships.*

Affirm

- *I am lovable; I am worthy.*

Move

- *Golden Lotus*

Next, do the Step Out of the Box, Open Your Heart and Mind movement as follows:

Intend

- *I intend to have positive, supportive, and loving relationships with men.*

Affirm

- *I am open to receiving love in my life.*

Move

- *Step Out of the Box, Open Your Heart and Mind*

Frightened?

James was 30 years old, articulate, and fulfilled in a comfortable job situation. When I asked him why he'd made an appointment for a session, he replied, "I thought it would be great to meet someone I can share my life with." Yet he'd never had a successful relationship; in fact, his experience was limited to a few fairly superficial dates.

When I watched James move, I noticed that he kept his chest closed while his arms pushed away what was in front of him. Yes, he *said* he wanted a relationship, but his body language told a different story. It was easy to see why James had no trouble getting women to go out with him on a first date—he was personable and attractive. But it was also easy to see why they soon stopped wanting to be with him—he was clearly reluctant to share who he was. For the woman across the dinner table from James, it must have been like talking to a sponge: He'd soak up everything he heard, but offer nothing in return. Pretty soon, she'd stop offering anything either, and a short time after that, she'd stop returning his calls.

I told James that his movements showed him to be a grounded person, and I asked him if he was willing to be more open. He said he'd like to try. As we ended the session, I gave this nice young man a hug. He almost seemed to shudder, drawing back and freezing to the spot. He was clearly taken aback, but it made him think. "I'd like to be able to accept that sort of gesture one day," he said.

Since James was so well grounded, I felt that our focus should be on opening his chest and arms, creating a place people could enter, so we began to work on that at his very next session. It was clear that he was ready for transformation, and it took almost no time for him to catch on to the bodymind connection. Here's the Moving Affirmation James put together:

 Intend

- *I intend to be open to a significant romantic relationship.*

Affirm

- *I can accept a supporting and loving partner into my life.*
- *I deserve love in my life.*

 Move

- *Step Out of the Box, Open Your Heart and Mind*

James had met a woman the week before he first came to see me. When he left the studio after our second session, he phoned her. As of this writing, they're still together—and James is still doing his Moving Affirmations.

Unable to Commit?

Barry had cold feet. He was in a relationship with a woman who loved him very much, and he loved her, too—but when the marriage question came up, Barry stalled. He couldn't bring himself to say yes; he was commitment-shy.

In Barry's case, the hesitation was understandable. He'd been married once before, and just as the marriage began to sour, his wife had become ill. Although Barry was no longer in love with his wife, he felt obligated to stay with her. Four years of suffering followed—for both of them—and then Barry's wife died. The experience left him sad, guilty, and very wary of becoming deeply involved again.

I saw this reluctance when Barry did the Wood movement. He dragged his feet and kept looking back to where he'd just been. Although his heart may have been open, he was stuck in the past, and there was no way he could move forward with his life. When I told Barry what I saw and suggested that he was still caught up in his former experience, his face took on a look of utter amazement as the bright light of clarity switched on. "Are you willing to let go of the past?" I asked him. "Are you ready to break free so that you can make choices in the present?"

Barry nodded. "Of course," he said. "That's why I'm here."

We worked on changing his steps in the Wood movement, practicing until Barry could keep his face forward while he brought both feet along. In addition, I had Barry do the Gold movement, focusing on bringing in possibilities from both sides.

Barry's intention in the Moving Affirmations was very strong—he really wanted to be present in his life—so it didn't take long. Within a couple of weeks, he was able to free himself of the shackles of the past. His relationship blossomed, and he was soon engaged.

But that wasn't all—Barry thrived at work, too. Clearly, the burden of his past had also been holding him back at the office. But no more—he became one of his company's most valuable employees.

Here's how Barry freed himself from old baggage and opened himself to real commitment:

Intend

- *I intend to let go of the past and be present in the now.*

Affirm

- *I release the chains of my past experiences.*
- *I am open to what is right for me now.*

Move

- *Wood*

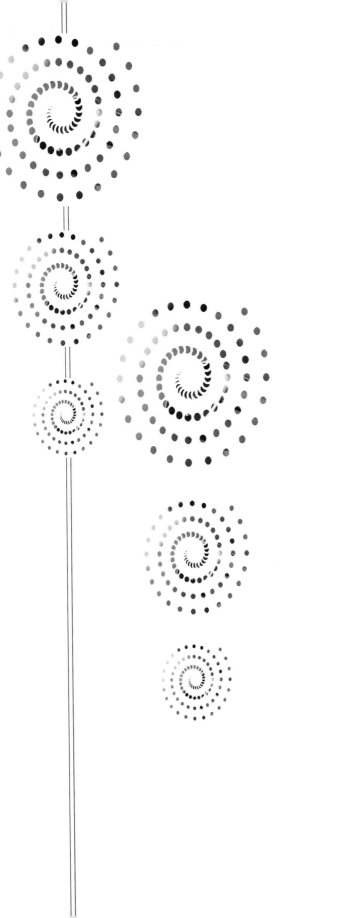

Chapter Eleven
Healing a
Relationship

"The ultimate test of a relationship

is to disagree but hold hands."

— Alexandra Penney

There's an advanced branch of Tai Ji practice known as *Tui Shou* (a word that translates as "push hands") that's actually a martial art. It combines the classic postures of Tai Ji—basically, the movements you've been learning in this book—and physical combat. In Tui Shou competitions, highly skilled contestants are pitted against one another in fast, fierce fighting matches. Victory goes to the combatant who knocks the other off center, often causing him or her to fall. There's a clear winner—and a clear loser.

Since that's definitely *not* what we're after in this chapter on healing relationships, you're probably wondering why we're discussing it at all. Well, a lot of relationships are not unlike encounters between rivals: Love affairs, marriages, friendships, employer/employee interactions, and parent/child relationships can all turn into power games or deteriorate into competitions. They can even become downright adversarial—a matter of tallying scores and keeping track of who's ahead and who's behind.

I'm not going to teach you how to "win" in a fight with your partner; instead, I'm going to turn Tui Shou on its head and make it the core of a set of movements for healing your relationship. It may sound illogical at first, but allow me to explain: At the heart of the practice is the principle that if you yield to a push, listen to the energy behind it, and follow it, you can make use of its force, remain centered, and send the energy pushing back. That's why there's no resistance in Tui Shou, no immovable stances, no aggressive counterattacks. If you're pressured on the left, you empty the left; and if you're pressured on the right, you empty the right.

Consider this concept: If you meet hard with soft, then you neutralize the hard. If you can go *with* the push instead of resisting it, then you can stay balanced and respond from your center. So by being sensitive to opposing energy, you can absorb the brunt of its force and let it flow right back to where it came from.

In the partner movements I've devised, however, there are no opponents and no attacks. Instead, the goal is for both individuals to learn to be sensitive to each other's energy. Each person must follow where the other leads, and both have the responsibility to respond from their own centers. The objective isn't to *overcome*, but to *come over* to one another, creating a mutual center where the relationship can flourish.

Perhaps it's not surprising that many couples tend to resist the responsibility the movements place on them and the constant contact they require. After all, it's human nature to assume that a troubled relationship is the other person's fault. And that also makes it easy, since it absolves each person of any responsibility for fixing the problem. But in the partner movements adapted from Tui Shou, *both* parties have to take responsibility for what's not working.

Ironically, what you blame your partner for doing is almost always a clue to your own conduct or demeanor. We humans tend to project onto others the very behaviors that bother us about ourselves, so what you see in others is almost always a reflection of who *you* are. That's why when you're happy, you tend to meet a lot of happy people. But when you're depressed, nothing seems to go right, and everyone seems to be difficult, as if your feelings were a magnet drawing more gloom your way.

In my days in the advertising business, for example, I seemed to only meet pushy and aggressive people. I'd shake my head in amazement that people could be so intense and meddlesome. But times have changed for me, and the people I meet today are kind and supportive. I've even found that some of the folks I once thought were brash and intrusive have become easygoing and helpful. How did it happen? Clearly, the "pushy" people I used to know didn't all undergo personality transplants, and the nice people I now meet didn't spring suddenly out of the earth—*I* changed. I was the one who was once pushy and aggressive, and those were the people I attracted or the qualities I brought out in others. I like to think that the warm, caring friends I have now are a reflection of the person I've become. As Henry David Thoreau once wrote, "Things do not change; we change."

You'll find that the partner movements I've adapted from Tui Shou hold an absolutely neutral, objective, and unequivocally accurate mirror up to you and your relationship. They'll show both of you where your responsibilities lie. More often than not—and whether you like it or not—these movements will bring startling clarity to your understanding of what's wrong in the relationship. I've seen it happen time after time.

You may find that the blame game begins as soon as you start the movements. And of course blaming doesn't work, because it's just a convenient way of not looking at the things you don't like about yourself. But the movements I've created won't let you get away with that; they'll force you to recognize precisely what each of you is doing to negatively affect the relationship.

The great thing is that once you both see the cause of your struggle defined and articulated in body language, simply shifting your moves will begin the healing process. Certainly, you can also analyze the whys and wherefores, but the point is that you don't *have to* do that analysis to begin the mending. Movement brings awareness, and awareness turns movement into therapy.

So make the shift, and practice the following movements. As awareness affects practice, practice also reinforces awareness, and doing these movements with your partner—even for just a few minutes each day—will make you more sensitive to each other for the remaining 23-plus hours. When each of you is willing to take responsibility for your own behavior, you can heal your relationship, strengthen it, and make it yield all the rich rewards human beings naturally seek from one another.

Your Mutual Center

Being centered is essential to doing the partner exercises in this chapter, but equally important is locating the mutual center you and your partner share. Here's how you'll do it:

(a) First Move

(b) Final Move

Instructions for
Your Mutual Center

(a) Face each other, each from your own center. In other words, stand center-to-center. Extend your arms, parallel to the ground, and touch fingertips. You've created a circle. *See* the circle in your mind's eye, and imagine its center.

(b) Release your left arms to your sides, and let the fingertips of your right hands touch each other at the center of the circle.

This is your mutual center, your relationship's center. If I were to take a aerial photo of the two of you at this moment, you'd see that your bodies form the yin-yang symbol.

The exercises in this chapter will take you through all three centers—yours, your partner's, and your mutual center—as you strengthen your ability to trust one another, communicate, and learn how to give and receive. They'll help you define what your separate and shared responsibilities are.

As with the Moving Affirmations, there are no "rules" for doing the partner exercises, but here are some guidelines to keep in mind:

- Stay centered.

- Stay in contact.

- Don't stay stuck in a position that doesn't work for you.

- Keep breathing.

- Keep your center and heart open to your partner.

- For the exercises that ask one of you to act as leader, while the other acts as follower, be sure to do the exercise a second time and switch roles.

- If an exercise requires that you begin with your right foot forward and left foot back, be sure to do it a second time with your left foot forward and right back. And change the position of your arms accordingly.

Are you ready? Then take your partner by the hand and let's begin.

Trust

Nothing is more basic to a relationship than trust. In the words of British novelist Graham Greene: "It is impossible to go through life without trust: that is to be imprisoned in the worst cell of all, oneself."[5] And of course there can be no relationship at all unless we emerge from the cell of ourselves. But just as trust can be lost, it can also be regained.

To help you establish or rebuild the trust that's so essential to every relationship, practice the movement exercise I call *Being Together*. It's about each of you letting the other be him- or herself, and fully accepting each other as you are. It's aimed at letting you discover whether or not you're in touch with one another—and at bringing you into closer communication.

Here's how it goes:

Being Together

Preview of Complete Movement

Step-by-Step

(a) First Move

(b) Second Move

(c) Third Move

(d) Final Move

Instructions for Being Together

(a) Face each other—center-to-center. One of you starts off as leader, so decide who will lead first. The leader raises her arms at approximately chest level, with palms down. Remember to keep your arms relaxed and soft. The follower raises his arms with palms down on top of the leader's hands. The follower's eyes are closed.

Slowly at first, the leader moves her arms up, down, in, and out as the follower maintains contact. The leader's movements take on a smooth rhythm, even as the movements become more elaborate—her arms may wave, or she may bend and dip. The leader should move as the spirit dictates.

(b) (c) (d) Still moving her arms, the leader may also begin to move her feet, stepping forward, back, and to the side.

When the leader feels that it's time to shift roles, and when both partners are facing each other center-to-center—bring your palms together at heart level. That's the signal to the follower to open his eyes and take up the role of leader. Without losing hand-to-hand contact, the new leader now extends his arms with palms down, and the follower places her hands, palms down, on the leader's hands. Her eyes are now closed.

Do the movement for as long as it feels right.

Do you see the element of trust in action here? It's up to the follower, with eyes closed, to maintain contact with the leader's hands, to bend when the leader bends, and to take a step when the leader takes a step. It's up to the leader to make this a conversation, to pull no tricks—no quick drops or fast pull-aways. If you do lose the connection, *make no judgments*. Just come back together and keep going.

· · · ᵃ · · ·

The Being Together exercise is an excellent barometer of how in touch you are as a team, and it certainly provided a revelation to Alan and Lois. When Lois was the leader, she wasn't able to trust the light touch of Alan's hand on top of hers. She wasn't convinced he could follow, so she held on to his fingers. In response, Alan simply dropped his arms.

"Do you notice what's happening?" I asked them. They did notice, and both admitted that it was an exact reflection of their relationship. Lois felt forced to always take the initiative even though she didn't want to. Alan didn't like it much when she took over, but since he never took charge himself, Lois stepped into what she saw as a vacuum. Alan, in turn, felt pushed around, so he simply forfeited the game—dropping his arms and ending contact.

When Alan was the leader, Lois wouldn't follow. "People won't lead if you don't follow," I suggested to her. I also reminded Alan that blaming Lois was a cop-out from taking any responsibility for the conversation between them. Awareness was the trigger for change, and the key for Alan and Lois was to stay centered and relaxed and then move from the center. That way, both partners could be open to possibilities well beyond "push" and "resist."

Alan and Lois began the movement again, this time with Alan as leader. Lois was now able to allow Alan to initiate moves. Her eyes were closed, but her awareness was now wide open, and by moving from her center, she could follow where he went. When Lois was leader, Alan stayed with her. Both became more receptive, and smiles appeared on faces that had only frowned before.

The two partners were thrilled. Alan felt empowered; for he saw that taking responsibility allowed him to influence the conversation. Lois was glad not to have to be in charge all the time—a learned behavior she'd long found burdensome. It was a powerful demonstration of how awareness can act as a bolt of lightning in the body—not just in the mind—changing the entire tone of their bodies' "conversation," opening communication that had been closed, and replacing misunderstanding with trust. The two continued to work on the movement at home, and in due course, I saw them relating to each other in a graceful conversation in which they were always in touch with one another, leading and following in perfect trust.

Communicate

Relationships are all about communication: two people making themselves known to one another. Relationships in trouble tend to be those where communication has broken down in some way. That breakdown reveals itself vividly—often starkly—when couples begin to do the partner movement aimed at opening and strengthening communication.

I call this next exercise *Hearing from Your Center*. In it, you'll share from the core of your energy and from your heart, and you'll move rhythmically and joyously. You've probably heard it said that sometimes words get in the way of true communication. Well, when you're hearing from your center, there are no words. Here's how it works:

Hearing from Your Center

Preview of Complete Movement

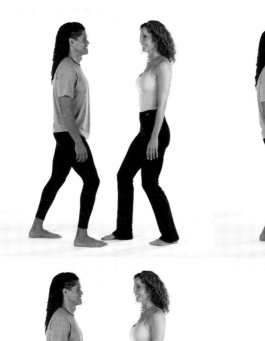

Step-by-Step

(a) First Move

(b) Second Move

(c) Third Move

(d) Final Move

Instructions for Hearing from Your Center

(a) Stand center-to-center, with your right foot forward and your left foot back. Relax and keep your knees soft so that you won't lose you balance when you begin to move. Remember to stay connected to the ground, and find your mutual center. Next, connect your right hands together with fingertips touching lightly. Then release the physical connection (hand-to-hand), but maintain your emotional connection.

(b) The leader moves forward from her center, feet flat on the ground, while the follower receives the energy and moves back.

(c) The leader then moves back to the starting position . . .

(d) . . . and now the other person initiates the forward motion.

Get into a rhythm. One forward, the other back—both of you mirroring each other and listening to each other through your centers. Don't try to predict when your partner will move; instead, just be open to listening from you center, and trust that your center can "hear."

After a while, the leader can take two steps forward (the follower will take two steps back), stop, and return to the forward-and-back rhythm of Step **(b)**. When the follower is ready, it's his turn to step forward two steps, then return to the standing-still rhythm. Eventually, you'll walk three, five, or ten steps—however many your physical space allows. The movement becomes a dance of connection.

One very important reason why the Hearing from Your Center dance strengthens communication is that it's *fun*. It really is a connecting dance that makes both partners happy, which is why it worked so well for George and Gary.

George and Gary had been referred to me by the couples therapist with whom they'd been working for some time, and it was clear from their serious demeanor that they were intensely focused on making their relationship work.

Perhaps they were *too* intense—for as I watched George and Gary execute the Hearing from Your Center dance, their concentration was dramatically evident. Desperate not to hurt one another, they both backed off any movement that might possibly throw the other off balance. Neither was willing to make the first move without instruction from me, and neither really accepted the forward movement of the other. Instead, they withdrew

and backed away. Clearly, neither man could read the other, and neither could follow where the other led.

I interrupted their movement and suggested that they were pussyfooting around one another. George and Gary appeared stunned and astonished at first, but both admitted that they knew they did this in life—and that they were finding it tiresome. It was taking a lot of energy to try to read each other all the time, and yet since both men were unable to understand what the other was feeling, neither knew how to respond. The result was that they tiptoed around each other's feelings and never really expressed their own emotions. As their movements showed, George and Gary weren't communicating to the other who they were and what they really wanted.

For the remainder of that session, we worked on getting both of them grounded in their own individual centers. From there, we found their mutual center and moved through it toward one another. I assigned them the Hearing from Your Center movement as their "homework," and when they returned to the studio the following week, the difference was immediately apparent—both in the joyous dance they shared and in their easier, more relaxed attitudes. Clearly, what they were learning in movement they were also applying in life, and they'd found true center-to-center communication.

• • • ° • • •

Helen and Paul suffered from an obvious case of communication breakdown. For years they'd been in couples therapy, trying to get to the heart of Helen's complaint that Paul never communicated. When they came to me, I asked them to do a simple movement I call *Listening from the Palm:*

Listening from the Palm

Preview of Complete Movement

Step-by-Step

(a) First Move

(b) Second Move

(c) Final Move

Instructions for
Listening from the Palm

(a) Stand center-to-center, right foot forward, left foot back. Stay relaxed and keep your knees soft so that you won't lose your balance. Find your mutual center and touch right palms.

(b) (c) The leader moves forward, shifting to her front foot and pushing with her palm (but sending energy from her center), while her partner receives the movement and moves back, putting more weight on his back foot. The leader then returns through the neutral position as the other person initiates the forward motion. Establish a flowing rhythm: one forward, the other back; mirroring each other and listening through your centers.

Since Helen was the partner complaining about a lack of communication, it was ironic that it was she who kept pulling away from Paul's forward push in the Listening from the Palm movement. In fact, each time he came forward, she turned sideways, taking her center right away from the space Paul was entering. After a while, Paul simply lost interest in doing the movement.

"Can you see what's wrong?" I asked the two of them. Paul responded first. He knew that something wasn't right, and he could pinpoint the moment when things started to go wrong. But he couldn't articulate what the "wrong" thing was.

I told them to try the movement again, and I asked Paul to let me know as soon as he felt that they were no longer on the right track. So they went through it again, and Paul stopped exactly when Helen's body turned away. The message Helen's body was transmitting came through loud and clear: Every time Paul tried to communicate, she made herself unavailable.

Helen was shocked. "I'm always direct in my communication!" she insisted.

"You're direct in *giving* communication, but are you equally direct in *receiving* it?" I asked. The question stunned her, yet to her credit, she saw the truth encoded in her body's movement. She saw that by taking her center away from Paul, the "direct" communication she thought she was giving was rendered meaningless. No wonder Paul was flummoxed.

We shifted the movement, and instantly, Paul and Helen were smiling at each other. The effect was dramatic, and as they practiced the movement in the days that followed, they also noticed some big changes at home—emotionally, spiritually, and sexually. Practicing the exercise allowed for the shift in behavior, and this shift made the exercise more joyful. They replaced an old pattern with the new one and strengthened their intimacy.

For Alan and Lois, the couple who practiced the Being Together movement, Listening from the Palm began as more of an arm-wrestling match than a partner movement. Lois's forward movement came from her arm, not from her center, and it was a vigorous shove. Since Alan wasn't receiving from center, the force of the push went right against his upper body, and his own arm automatically resisted. "See?" he said. "She's always pushing me around." What should have been a body-to-body conversation had become a shouting match. You know the expression about a situation being so noisy you can't hear yourself think? That's what was happening with Alan and Lois.

First, I showed Alan what to do when he felt pushed too hard. "Don't resist the push," I told him. "Instead, absorb it." By moving *with* the push, in best Tui Shou fashion, I showed Alan how to deepen the bend in his knees and bend his arm back into his body while keeping his feet on the ground. "Feel the push coming in," I told him. "Let its energy move down your body into the earth, which can absorb it." Then, as the movement flowed back, Alan could feel the energy move back up his body and out toward Lois.

Alan tried it, and it worked. In fact, it worked so well that Lois almost felt pushed over—partly from the energy Alan was reflecting, and partly out of sheer surprise at his new-found dynamism. So I showed her how to do the same thing—to receive the energy of the push down into her body and into the ground, and to let it ride back up her body and out toward Alan.

The two couldn't have been happier. Just as the Being Together movement helped them open a connection of trust, Listening from the Palm was creating an energetic body-to-body conversation between dynamic equals. They were learning how to communicate—and they liked it.

Give and Receive

Just as you must pump a well in order to draw water, so must you give love in order to make it flow back to you. Giving and receiving are two sides of one coin—the yin and yang in perpetual motion—and that's what relationships are all about. Here's an exercise call the *Yin-Yang Circle*, which will show how well you give *and* receive in your relationship; practicing it will help you do both better:

Yin-Yang Circle

Preview of Complete Movement

Step-by-Step

(a) First Move

(b) Second Move

(c) Third Move

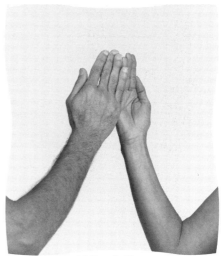

(d) Fourth Move

Step-by-Step

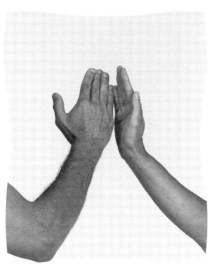
(e) Fifth Move

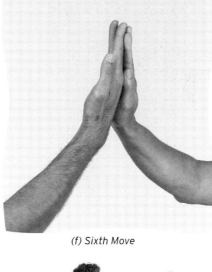
(f) Sixth Move

(g) Seventh Move

(h) Final Move

Instructions for Yin-Yang Circle

(a) Face your partner, centers aligned, with your right foot forward and your left foot back. Extend your arms outward, parallel to the ground, in a relaxed fashion. With your palms open, touch your partner's hands, thus creating a natural circle.

Now release your left arms and touch right hands at the center of the circle you just created—at your mutual center. (Remember forming the yin-yang symbol when you did the exercise to find your mutual centers? This is the same position.)

(b) (c) (d) (e) (f) Keeping in mind the circle you just formed, the leader pushes forward, her palm facing her partner's heart. The yang is going toward the receiving yin, and now the follower rolls his hand over to receive the yang with the back of his hand, yielding to the leader's open palm. Put another way, the follower's palm is open toward his own heart.

When the yang has gone as far as possible . . .

(g) (h) . . . to the edge of the imaginary circle—it must reverse and receive. Now the follower's palm opens, facing the leader's heart. The leader's palm rolls over as she shifts into yin, and the back of her palm yields and brings in the follower's yang.

In this exercise, each of you is letting the other into your space—from one's center, through the mutual center, and into the territory of the other's center. You're inviting each other into your lives, and—just as important—you're open to entering into each other's lives. As you push forward, you'll want your partner to receive you fully; when you feel that happening, you'll know that your partner is reciprocating and that you share a real relationship.

That's why doing this exercise can reveal so much about the quality of giving and receiving between two people. I've seen partners pushing forward only halfway, as if they don't want to be fully received. I've seen people who are unable to open their palms toward their partners' hearts, but when I showed them what they were doing, they were able to shift their movements and salvage their relationship.

• • • ᵒ • • •

Jeff and Leslie were a very loving couple, a walking advertisement for opposites who attract. Jeff was a muscular, athletic guy who'd once won a varsity letter in wrestling and spoke in a booming baritone voice. Leslie was a delicate—almost fragile—ballerina who talked in a near-whisper. Given the difference in their physical sizes, I suppose it wasn't surprising to see Jeff take hold of Leslie's palm as she was receiving. He was trying to help her, of course—he thought that he was "taking care of things" for her. He did it gently, out of love—but the effect was an interference. By pulling Leslie's hand toward himself, Jeff was determining how much and when she could move, and he was making assumptions about her and acting *for* her; in a very real sense he was controlling her. Leslie, in turn, was letting him take charge; her assumption was that such control made Jeff happy, so she submitted out of love.

But making assumptions isn't communicating, and submission isn't giving or receiving. Jeff and Leslie loved each other, but neither was giving what the other needed, and neither was getting what they wanted. As a couple, they had difficulty making any joint decisions because they were both trying to guess what would make the other happy.

It was up to both of them to shift the pattern—up to Jeff to be aware of his movement and to stop being a buffer between Leslie and life, and up to Leslie to stop allowing him to determine what she could receive. They practiced the Yin-Yang Circle at the end of every workday. As they did the movement, they talked together about the events of the day, and the conversation moved with the rhythm of their bodies.

As time passed, Leslie and Jeff found that they were getting better and better at saying exactly what they wanted. They understood that too much controlling "care" actually cut them off from their true needs, and they learned that expressing themselves clearly was a true measure of love. Ultimately, wrestler and dancer—yin and yang—really did complete each other.

Talking while doing the partner exercises may sound strange, but in fact, it's a fine idea—provided you don't talk about the movements themselves or criticize the way either one of you does them. That kind of conversation is off-limits. But any other topic is okay, and the process of exchanging thoughts during the movements can be downright beneficial, as two of my clients, Steve and Diana, learned.

For Steve and Diana, the issue was that neither felt comfortable sharing their feelings—at least, that was Diana's version of the situation. Steve had agreed to come to my studio to see if they couldn't resolve their communication issues. After spending three sessions on grounding them in their individual centers, I asked them to do the Yin-Yang Circle.

Their discomfort was palpable. Neither was able to receive very well, and each was sure that the other was at fault. I could see them concentrating, and I noticed the strain as each pushed forward toward the other's space against an invisible barrier. I called a halt to the exercise and made a suggestion. "Try it again," I said. "Only this time, each time you go forward, say whatever it is you feel at that moment about your partner."

They seemed a little hesitant, but they positioned their feet, touched hands, and began. Steve pushed forward first. "I admire who you are as a person," he told Diana. She seemed startled.

"Oh, well . . . uh . . . what?" she fumbled. She couldn't quite receive what he'd said; instead, she deflected it, saying nothing when it was her turn to push forward and give.

Steve spoke again. "Your eyes are beautiful right now," he said. Diana softened, and she received Steve into her space. She seemed worried that she had nothing to say, so I advised her to "just wait until the words come." Eventually, they did.

"Steve," she said at last, "I'm really impressed that you were willing to come here and do these sessions."

"You always have good ideas," Steve answered.

"You're so graceful when you do this," Diana returned.

Their bodies now moved in rhythm. Both were giving and receiving, and both were getting feedback. They weren't just saying nice things because they'd been instructed to do so; they were opening their hearts to each other and letting the bodymind lead them. They focused on all of the positive aspects of their relationship. It was something of a lovefest, and to an observer, it was beautiful.

Other Relationships

You don't have to be in love to want to make a relationship work better. You can do all these exercises with friends, family members, anyone with whom you interact—any relationship that needs healing.

I've also put these exercises to good use in the corporate arena. It makes sense: Teamwork is highly prized in corporate organizations, yet competitiveness is so pervasive in that culture that it's often difficult to maintain a spirit of cooperation. My seminars bring together people from all levels of the hierarchy to practice trust, communication, and the giving and receiving that are essential when people work together.

Individual managers can also use these movement exercises to improve the way they relate to the people who work for them—it's in their self-interest to do so. The people who work for them are the ones who are going to help them succeed.

Better relationships make life better everywhere. Create a positive intention together, and let these movement exercises take you there.

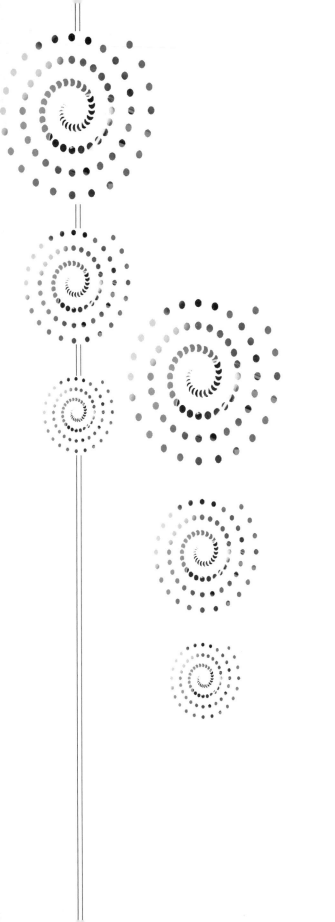

Chapter Twelve

The Dance of Fire: Bringing Passion and Excitement (Back) into a Relationship

"A successful marriage is an edifice

that must be rebuilt everyday."

— André Maurois

*W*ant to improve your sex life? Who doesn't?! If sex with your lover has become predictable, routine, or infrequent, or if you've ever experienced sexual incompatibility with a partner, then you'd certainly welcome new passion into your life. Even if you enjoy robust physical intimacy on a regular basis, you probably wouldn't mind enjoying it more.

But sex is a complex process—on the physiological plane alone, it involves networks of interrelated actions and reactions involving the neurological, vascular, and endocrine systems of the body. On a mental and emotional level, you and your partner are also affected by your individual attitudes, needs, and responses, which have been shaped by your personal history, family, social and religious beliefs, and past romantic experiences. As if that weren't enough, a host of external factors—such as illness, fatigue, and stress—can all affect what goes on in the bedroom. So there could be any number of reasons for your dissatisfaction.

Whatever the cause, the solution isn't just trying a new physical technique, or bending your body into the "secret" positions depicted on the crumbling walls of some archaeological site. Lovemaking is more than a function of the sex organs; it's about being connected in the deepest possible way. (That's why people say that the brain is the most powerful erogenous zone.) In Tai Ji, we put it this way: Sex works best and is most satisfying when there's a connection through all three centers—head, heart, and tantien—as well as a couple's mutual center.

All of the partner exercises you learned in Chapter 11 will help move you toward this goal—especially if you do them with the intention of enhancing your sexual pleasure as part of healing your relationship.

When the Spark Has Died Down

Sam and Sarah had one of the most common complaints I hear in my practice. They'd been married for 15 years when they came to my studio, and they were as "normal" a couple as you could find (if there is such a thing). Sam and Sarah each had fulfilling careers, along with two kids, a dog, and a lovely home in a quiet neighborhood. Like all couples, they'd had their ups and downs over the years, but they were committed to one another and their marriage, and they'd become accustomed to one another's personality quirks.

However, the spark had gone out of their relationship—sex had become predictable. Sam and Sarah found that between maintaining a household, dealing with office politics, and chauffeuring the kids from school to soccer practice, physical intimacy didn't seem worth the effort. Still, they knew that their relationship was missing something important, and while they had no expectation of recapturing the excitement of their early courtship, they thought they ought to try to ignite a little more fire between them.

So the first thing I asked Sarah and Sam to do was the Yin-Yang Circle (see Chapter 11 for instructions). The "problem" was immediately evident: They didn't make eye contact, never moved their feet, and leaned indifferently in each other's direction from centers that were slightly askew. I was watching a dull conversation that had been saying the same thing over and over for years.

"Stop," I told them. "Let's try this instead." I instructed Sarah and Sam to go back to neutral (standing center-to-center, with right foot forward, left foot back) and touch right hands. "Now," I said, "instead of pushing forward and back, just move freely—however you want."

I suggested that they might move up, down, or sideways—as well as forward and back—and I told them to be free with their hands as well.

"Move however you want to," I instructed, "but keep moving, and *stay connected*. Think of communicating from your centers instead of using your eyes to see or your ears to hear. Leadership will shift as your movements shift," I told them. "The point is to perform your own free-form dance while keeping your partner involved."

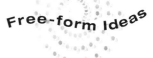
Free-form Ideas

So, tentatively and stiffly, Sam and Sarah began. At first they kept losing touch, and neither could follow very well. Each expected something of the other, so neither was fully present. It was like a conversation between people who weren't listening to one another—they were face-to-face, but their focus was somewhere else.

Frustrating though it was for Sam and Sarah, I asked them to keep at it. Their frustration eventually prompted them to focus their attention, and as they did so, their bodies relaxed. I could see them growing more alert—following one another not just with their eyes, but with their centers as well. Third eye, heart, and tantien—all key seats of the libido— were at last all coming into play. In effect, I was watching the creation of an intimate connection.

Since doing the Yin-Yang Circle in this free-form way wasn't predictable, neither partner could guess where the other was going—yet they had to follow. They found that this could only be done when their centers were attuned. And over time, the movement ignited a new level of passion and excitement in Sam and Sarah's relationship.

Yearning for a "Heartfelt" Relationship

In a curious and almost refreshing switch from the classic stereotype, David complained that all Mary wanted was sex. She had no interest in hugging or cuddling, and no patience for foreplay. When David said that he wanted a "heartfelt" relationship with Mary, it struck me as an eloquent plea for an intimate connection of centers.

Again, the Yin-Yang Circle movement etched the issue in sharp relief. As David moved forward in the movement, Mary consistently failed to turn her palm toward her own heart. Instead, she'd hold her hand out toward David, as if pushing him away and keeping him out of her heart. She even closed her eyes. When it was Mary's turn to move forward, she kept her palm open to David's heart, but she did the movement quickly and offhandedly—as if reluctant to enter deeper into the relationship.

The situation was clearly hard on David. He showed himself open and willing for Mary to come in as far as she could, yet she'd only come a small part of the way. He was eager to give, and she routinely rebuffed him. An open heart like David's could only take so much rejection and resistance, and as the three of us discussed the issue, it became clear that David was thinking seriously about leaving the relationship. This revelation surprised and chilled Mary; she'd had no idea that her relationship with David was in such peril. It made her sit up, take notice, and try to salvage the situation.

I offered Mary a possible solution: I explained that making a shift in movement could lead to a change in her life—and I told her in all honesty that the shift might not come easily or quickly. "But," I said, "we're alone in this room, just the three of us, and if you try to make the shift and can't, or don't like it once you've tried it, you're free to let it go. This is a safe space to give it a try." Mary nodded, and she and David did the Yin-Yang Circle again, this time equipped with new awareness about the movement and what it meant in their relationship.

Making the shift was difficult for Mary, and it didn't quite work at that session, nor at the next. But she persisted in trying, and David appreciated her effort. The first part of the shift was in her willingness to go closer to him, but she still had trouble letting him come toward her. Even when she was finally able to turn her palm open toward her own heart, she held it away from her body, as if she'd taken down a barrier but still needed to keep herself at a safe distance.

Then one day, Mary actually moved her open palm very near her heart, bringing David in closer than ever before. As she did, she began to cry and was unable to go on. The tears brought forth memories of more than one lover who'd left her feeling trampled, isolated, and fragile. A repeated pattern of such treatment had made Mary resolve never to be vulnerable again, and by closing off from intimacy, she believed she was protecting herself against another potentially negative experience.

Clearly, Mary needed to be comfortable moving from her own center before she could feel safe with David. So she decided to do some solo work with me, and we went through the Moving Affirmations to help her find her inner strength. At the same time, she and David continued to work on the Yin-Yang Circle and other partner exercises. As Mary grew more centered in her self, she was able to let David in even more, and their connection went deeper and grew stronger.

It took a lot of courage and commitment on both their parts, but they stayed with it. David had been encouraged by Mary's willingness to work on her issues, and now that Mary was adding heart and mind to their sexual activity—creating the "heartfelt" relationship David had longed for—sex was better for both of them. Mary discovered that underneath it all, the cuddling, hugging, and affection that David had missed were what she'd craved as well. It took a fair amount of work, but at last she was able to give that affection—and to receive it.

Bedroom as Battleground: The Control Issue

Tessa and Ed were veterans of 12 years of marriage. I use the word *veteran* intentionally, for when it came to sex, their relationship was more like making war than making love. Tessa, who harbored a real phobia about commitment, had dragged her heels about getting married in the first place, and Ed persisted in treating her like a princess even when she acted like a rat. Both sought control in the relationship, and the standoff was most vividly evident in the bedroom. In fact, their sexual relations had become so dysfunctional that Ed was practically impotent. They knew that they had to do something if they were going to stay together, so they came to me seeking help for what they called their "physical problems."

I asked them to do one of the partner movements, then another, and then another. Yet whatever the movement, Tessa continually chided Ed for "doing it wrong," so Ed kept dropping out of the exercise—"since nothing I do is right." I suggested that they both stop talking, but Tessa found that impossible. As she criticized, she pushed, and as she pushed, he pushed back. They were deadlocked, and they both looked tense and miserable.

"Is this what happens in bed?" I asked bluntly. The answer was a clear yes, so we went right back to basics—to the Being Together movement (see Chapter 11 for instructions).

At first Ed tried to go where he could get Tessa to follow. He had a preconceived idea of what she'd like, but he was invariably wrong. When Tessa was the leader, she tried to dictate Ed's movements, and he felt undermined by this and resented it. In other words, it was a clear reflection of their sexual relationship. They kept losing the connection with one another, and Tessa kept talking. Bottom line: They weren't really doing the movement, and they certainly weren't playing by the rules of the game. Ed and Tessa needed to let go and relinquish the struggle for control.

We tried the movement again, and this time I designated Ed as leader and Tessa as follower—and admonished her not to talk at all. "Let go," I told them both. "Let your centers lead you." Ed began slowly, with just his arms. He moved them up, down, out, then high up, then way down, and then in a waving motion. In order to follow his movements, Tessa had to move from her center, and this time, that's exactly what she did. They were face-to-face now, center-to-center. Ed began to move his feet, and lo and behold—Tessa moved with him. What's more, I could tell that she enjoyed it. Ed liked it, too, because for once he was being followed and not judged. He brought his palms together at heart level, signaling that Tessa should be leader, and she moved smoothly into the role. Now that she had learned to follow, she could also take responsibility for leading.

I could see that Ed and Tessa were truly beginning to make a shift. Clearly, they felt safer with each other through doing the Being Together movement; each felt listened to and in tune with the other. So I assigned them to do the exercise before making love.

Over the next several weeks, the impact on their sex life was dramatic: "Way better than having a few drinks," Ed joked. The simple movement had deepened their connection, and their performance had become more dance than exercise. They kept up the pattern for several months, during which time their problems in the bedroom yielded to exciting, fulfilling, loving physical intimacy. Ed and Tessa still do the exercises whenever they feel a need to renew their connection or enhance their sexual pleasure.

Passive Partner

One of the things that had so attracted Peter to Fran was her independent nature. Yet once they were married, she seemed to always go along with what he wanted.

"What movie would you like to see?" he'd ask.

Fran would answer: "Whichever one you want to see."

"Where shall we have dinner?"

"It doesn't matter; you decide," she'd reply. There was simply nothing behind Fran; she yielded to his every wish.

Peter wasn't happy in the marriage because he yearned for an equal partner, but Fran thought she was giving her husband what he wanted. Her mother had been of the school that taught that the woman should always defer to the man, and while Fran had rebelled against that idea most of her life, she succumbed to it when she got married. (We often mimic behaviors we disagree with if we don't know any other way to act.) Fran couldn't understand why her attempts to please Peter didn't satisfy him, so she wasn't happy either.

Of course, this pattern of behavior affected their sex life as well. Peter complained that Fran was just too passive, yet Fran said that she was acting out of love. Something had to change.

The first time Fran and Peter came to the studio, I asked them to go through a few of the partner movements. In every one of them, Fran was constantly being pushed off-center; she yielded, not *with* the movement, but in retreat. Her attention was on Peter's center, with no focus whatsoever on her own.

I knew we needed to get both Fran and Peter to focus on their own centers first, and then find their mutual center. After they'd done that, I assigned a variation of the Yin-Yang Circle. It goes like this:

Yin-Yang Circle Variation

Preview of Complete Movement

Step-by-Step

(a) First Move

(b) Second Move

(c) Third Move

(d) Fourth Move

(e) Fifth Move

(f) Final Move

Instructions for
Yin-Yang Circle Variation

(a) Face your partner, with your right foot forward and your left foot back. Extend your arms in a relaxed fashion, find your mutual center, and touch your right wrist bones back-to-back.

(b) The leader starts by moving forward on his right (front) leg, and the follower receives the movement. Do this back and forth in an easy rhythm, wrists still touching lightly.

(c) (d) (e) (f) When ready, the leader steps forward with his left (back) foot as his arm pushes, and then circles, the follower's arm. Receiving the move, the follower steps back with her right (forward) foot and maintains contact with the leader's circling arm. As always, reverse roles and repeat the exercise.

When comfortable with this single-step movement, add as many steps as you want—three, five, ten, and so on. In each case, return to the original nonstepping rhythmic back-and-forth movement before you reverse "leaders."

This movement was important for Peter and Fran because it required them to continually return to their own centers and focus on their mutual center—bringing balance back into their relationship.

When you create a circle together, then visualize your mutual center, you'll see that you can't have more yin than yang—or more yang than yin—in a relationship. The two must be in balance. You'll also recognize that each partner needs the other to complete the balance.

It took time for Peter and Fran to find such balance, but when they finally did, the movement became a graceful, sexy dance that was tremendous fun for them both. Their joy followed them into the bedroom as well—as each of them told me in separate phone calls.

Joy in Sex

Sadly, there are many people for whom sex is unfulfilling at best, joyless at worst. Statistics tell us that only about half of married women experience orgasm with regularity, and about a third of single women are consistently orgasmic with a partner—while an estimated one-quarter of all women (single or married) never or almost never experience orgasm. While there can be physical causes for orgasmic difficulties, the most common cause is psychological—a consequence of emotional baggage long carried.

I'd worked one-on-one with Gina for some time, and from the very beginning, I'd noted her reluctance to move her hands over any part of her body below her tantien center. She seemed shy about lowering her arms to the ground, and would regularly move her hands away from her center. In the Water movement, her arms would come down only so far, and in the Golden Lotus, she typically "forgot" to reach all the way down to the earth. In fact, in all her movements, Gina tended to avoid this part of her body.

Sensing Gina's discomfort, I was reluctant to broach the subject. But one day, as she worked on releasing stress through the Water movement, she broke through her usual reluctance and succeeded in bringing her arms down the length of her body. That move triggered a reaction in her, and as the tears flowed, we began to talk.

Sex was not an easy issue for Gina to discuss, and it never had been. She'd grown up in a home where sex was never mentioned, where physical demonstrations of affection were unheard of, and where the body was nothing more than something to be expensively clothed. The atmosphere in the family was cool, correct, and distant, and remaining "in control" was touted as a primary goal in life.

Gina's first experiment with sex hadn't been successful—she'd had an affair with a married man, which had left her feeling like a "dirty little secret." It reinforced her sense of shame, her inhibitions about her body, and her fear of losing control in some kind of physical and emotional intimacy she couldn't quite manage.

When I met Gina, she was living with a loving and patient man to whom she was extremely attracted, but she never achieved orgasm, and receiving even the slightest pleasure from sexual activity filled her with guilt.

Gina thought she was doomed to joyless sex forever, and that she simply lacked the potential to experience orgasm or an intimate connection with her partner. I was able to convince her that her problem was common, that clinical evidence was clear that most women *do* have the potential to experience orgasm, and that our work together could help. She was willing to give the movement therapy a try, so we got to work.

Two Moving Affirmations proved particularly important for Gina—the Water movement, to release stress and tension; and the Gold movement, to bring in the support she needed for healing. (The latter movement was particularly appropriate because it asks you to open at the hip—in the very area that Gina had so determinedly avoided.) Gina's eventual ability to shift that movement was the breakthrough that opened the door to connecting with her partner.

When Gina felt ready, we brought her boyfriend, Rob, into the picture. At the heart of their work together was the Yin-Yang Circle, in which we worked to get Gina comfortable opening all her centers to Rob. It took time—at first, Gina was able to open her mind and heart but not her tantien; instead, she would be rooted on both feet, just pushing her arms out from her shoulders, not from her center. Naturally, that meant that her reach was limited—from mind and heart as well as from tantien.

Going through these exercises with Rob made Gina confront the old inhibitions about her body, question her need for self-control, and move on from past sexual experiences. She and Rob had to work very hard at making their own center-to-center connection strong enough to unload the psychological baggage she'd been carrying since childhood, but fortunately, both were sufficiently committed to each other to stick it out, and today their relationship is better than ever. They recently married, and Gina has reported to me that she experiences orgasm with increasing frequency.

Gina and Rob are both grateful for the improvement, and they continue to work with me—aware that this deep-rooted problem won't be "solved" overnight. In fact, they've worked out a routine that I recommend to anyone interested in achieving or enhancing sexual pleasure:

First, they do the Just Being movement. This relaxes them both and opens each to the other. Then they do the Yin-Yang Circle, which enables them to connect across all their centers. Once connected, they turn the movement into a dance, bringing a sense of play to the practice.

As you do these and other movements to bring passion and excitement to your relationship, remember to create an intention with your partner. This will be a powerful force to support your potential to change. Do the movements with an open heart, an open mind, and an open body. And remember to breathe and enjoy.

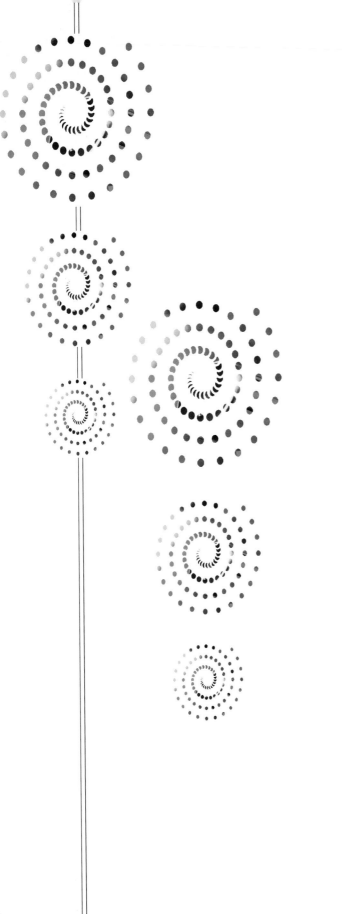

Chapter Thirteen

Letting Go:
Life Can
Be Good

"Try softer."

— Lily Tomlin

There's an old joke about a man who was hanging by his fingertips from a cliff 2,000 feet above the valley floor. Terrified, he looked to the top of the cliff and screamed: "Is there anyone up there who can help me?!" A deep, booming voice from on high answered: "Yes, I will help you. I am the Lord. Now just relax and let go." After a long pause, the man yelled out: "Is there anybody else up there?"

This chapter is about learning to trust the response from on high: It really is time to relax and let go.

Addicted to Growth

Alexandra was a tall and vibrant businesswoman. She pursued her career, her men, and her play with the same vigor and single-minded focus, and she reveled in being called extraordinary. Yet at the same time, she was exhausting–no one could keep up with her.

After some thorough soul-searching, Alexandra decided that personal growth would be her next pursuit. She wanted to be everything she could be, which was an admirable and lofty ideal. To achieve her goal, she attended workshops and seminars, worked with therapists, and studied with me for nearly a decade. Alexandra pursued growth with the same assiduous attention she'd devoted to her work and to her many other pursuits: She identified the issues in her life and systematically resolved each of them. Finally, she reached a place where all she was needed was maintenance.

But Alexandra couldn't stop improving herself. In a way, personal growth had become an addiction–she got high from the drama of finding and resolving a new issue. It's a great feeling to dig in to something and "fix" it, but after Alexandra had tackled the major issues of her life, she kept looking for more. All of a sudden, daily life seemed rife with problems that needed attention. For example, if she became even momentarily irritated with a rude checkout cashier at the supermarket, she took it as evidence of her personal inability to cope–and she set out to "cure" herself. Alexandra's addiction to personal growth had become a real problem in her life, and it showed.

Alexandra routinely did the ten Moving Affirmations at home, to the point that she could do every movement in her sleep. But in going through the sequence one day at my studio, she "forgot" the Flight of the Eagle, a movement that had always been a favorite of hers (which is more proof that this work isn't about just memorizing movements). Clearly, Alexandra's body was alerting her that there was an issue that needed examining, so we took some time to talk about it. Since she'd been doing the Moving Affirmations for so long, she knew that this was her body's way of telling her, "It's time to let go." She'd been on a mission, but her tasks were all accomplished. It was time to just *live*.

But there was another dimension to her problem: Like the guy hanging from the cliff wall, Alexandra was scared. If she stopped working on being extraordinary, she'd have no more excuses for *not* being extraordinary. (This showed up in the way Alexandra did the Golden Lotus movement—her "blossom" never fully opened.)

Well, to begin with, Alexandra *was* extraordinary—by every rational measurement. But of course, fear isn't rational. Somewhere in her youth, she'd been trained to think that life was about hard work. She'd been taught that she was somehow obligated to realize the potential of *all* of her gifts to the fullest, and that meant working hard. No one had ever told Alexandra that she could stop to enjoy the fruits of her labor, which is why Alexandra did *everything* intensely—until her mission became an addiction from which she needed to escape. The movement for her letting go was the Flight of the Eagle, accompanied by the following messages:

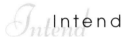 ## Intend

- *I intend to allow myself to experience the joy of life.*
- *I intend to feel free.*

 ## Affirm

- *It is time to let go and enjoy life.*

 ## Move

- *Flight of the Eagle*

In time, Alexandra became aware that she needed to, as Lily Tomlin's once said, "try softer." When she did, her spirit was freed and she began to soar.

Enjoying the View

I've had more than a passing acquaintance with Alexandra's "addiction"; I went through the same thing myself. There was a time, shortly after my epiphany at the Tai Ji workshop in New York, when I went after my own personal growth with a vengeance. I dealt with a number of issues that had plagued me, and I also worked hard with my husband, Michael, on our relationship.

Years of labor paid off, and Michael and I found ourselves at a wonderful place in our lives. We felt centered and grounded as individuals and as a couple. We'd come a long way. Arriving at that place should have been a signal to me to just live, to appreciate the place we were at and to engage its possibilities.

But while Michael got that signal, I missed it. I wanted to keep going, do more work, and look for more glitches. I knew that there were seminars out there, and workshops, research studies, articles, and books that would help me identify yet more life issues I could try to fix.

"Can't we just rest and enjoy each other for a while?" Michael asked me. It was so simple, and yet it had never occurred to me! I agreed to suspend my need to "fix things" constantly—even obsessively. I allowed myself the time to enjoy the fruits of all that we had done, time to feel free and joyous. Together, my husband and I took the time to rest and be in the present.

The movement that helped me was Return to Mountain. It let me sit quietly and savor the beautiful view available to me from the place where I had arrived. My intention was: "I intend to enjoy the place I have arrived at." My affirmation was: "I love my life right now."

Of course, I'm still not "done"; as in every life, issues continue to surface. But now I'm able to address the conflicts that arise from a place of rest and strength. That's been an important lesson for me.

Letting Go: The Process

When you need to release, focus on the Flight of the Eagle movement. Either do the movement all by itself—and really feel the sense of soaring—or do it in the context of other Moving Affirmations, but really focus on it.

To concentrate on Flight of the Eagle does not mean, however, that you need to give up other movements. In fact, at no time should you ever give up the other movements entirely. After all, nothing is ever really "cured" for good. Issues that have surfaced and been dealt with can resurface; issues that never played a role in your life can suddenly require attention. So even if you're dealing with another issue in your life, you can still focus on the need to let go through the Flight of the Eagle.

How long should you do it? As with all of these movements, there's no clock. When you feel a lightening of the load, you'll know that you've "solved" the letting-go issue.

Another movement that can be useful in the letting-go process is called *Wakame*. You might recognize the name as Japanese for "seaweed." In fact, wakame is kelp, and in the Wakame movement, your body acts like a long leaf of kelp in an underwater forest. Imagine such a forest, and picture yourself as a part of it. Your feet stay rooted to the seabed while your body moves with the currents, waving back and forth as they surge and ebb. When the tide subsides, you reach toward the sun, the center of the universe.

In all martial arts—and certainly in Tai Ji—the successful warrior is the one who can let go and be fully relaxed. Release totally and relax fully. Be a fresh, green frond of kelp swaying in the currents of a deep-blue ocean.

The Wakame movement is a great way to let go, and it's also a wonderful self-massage. Many of my students make it the warm-up exercise before they begin their Moving Affirmations because it helps them relax and stay grounded. When you let go with Wakame, you're really ready for anything life has to offer.

Wakame

Preview of Complete Movement

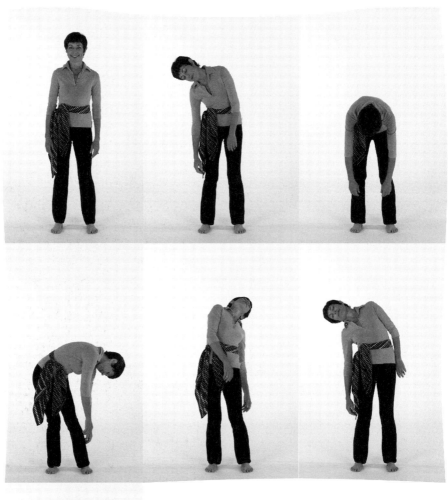

Step-by-Step

(a) First Move

(b) Second Move

(c) Third Move

(d) Fourth Move

(e) Fifth Move

(f) Sixth Move

(g) Final Move

Go Ahead, Fly Free

You're very near the end of this book, and chances are you've done a lot of work on yourself already. You've released many of the patterns that have held you back from real-izing your full potential, and you've learned that you *can* rewrite your story. That's a lot to have done. So before you go any further, remember to take some time to feel free and joyous, and listen to that voice from on high urging you to "just relax and let go." Let your-self experience the gains you've already made, and the fullness of who you are.

The Chinese phrase *wu wei* translates, more or less, as "going with the flow." When you learn to feel centered, when you can trust the essential you, and when you can release the need to struggle, then you'll have graduated to wu wei.

There's a story of an old man who fell off a ledge into a pool beneath an enormous and powerful waterfall. A renowned guru and his disciples were meditating nearby, and they ran to help the man. As they drew near, they saw him being tossed, tumbled, and submerged every which way by the overwhelming force of the cascade. Yet by the time they reached him, he'd emerged from the water and was drying himself off by the side of the pool. The guru and his disciples were stunned.

"How were you able to make it through that water?" the guru asked. "No one could survive under such pounding pressure. What is your secret?"

The old man said quietly, "There is no secret. I learned when I was very young to just let the water take me where it will. I don't fight it, and I don't struggle against its power. I just let go. It always works."[6]

All of us can learn from the old man. We need to discover when to "hang tough" and when to just let go and "wu wei" in our lives.

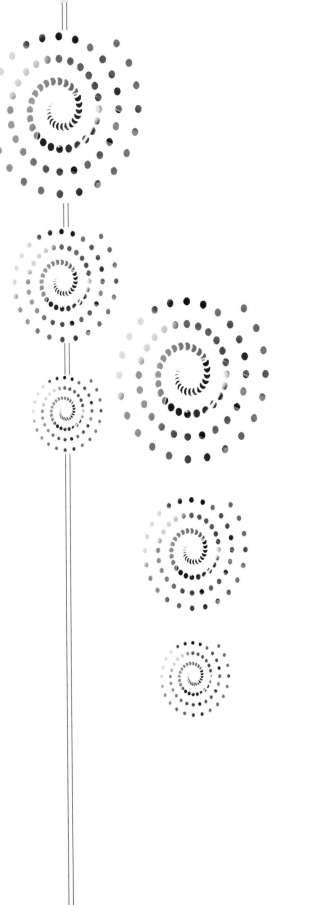

Chapter Fourteen

It's a Journey—
Enjoy It!

"Every step of the journey is the journey."

— Zen wisdom

$\mathcal{W}$e live in a society of fast food and sound bites, where everything is supposed to happen immediately. We've come to expect instantaneous results in everything—from drive-through banking and online medical diagnoses to our own personal growth. That's why so many self-help books are disappointing: They promise a magic remedy that will bring about instant change.

This book is different. *Every Move You Make* isn't about magic; it's about taking charge of your life in a new way, freeing yourself from self-imposed limits, letting go of burdens, finding your own anchor, and creating the life you want to live—and chances are that none of these things will happen in the blink of an eye.

The fact is, whatever you're trying to change probably took a long time to get that way, so it will likely take a long time to *un*-get that way. The first step is to identify the pattern of behavior, then you must choose to change it and conscientiously commit to doing whatever work is required.

The exercises and movements in this book are aimed at letting you see the potential for a new way of being—after all, every old habit must be replaced with a new one. But you can't command the change to occur all at once, like a drill sergeant ordering an inexperienced recruit to "drop down and give me ten—on the double." Instead, you must give yourself time—time for your body to absorb the shift, and time for the shift to translate to your mind, spirit, and behavior.

Making the Shift: Four Stages

Expect to go through all four of these stages in the process of change:

1. *Inspiration.* You'll discover new possibilities in the movements. A click will go off in your head, you'll feel your body set itself in motion, or you'll experience a moment of true awareness—what the Zen Buddhists call *satori*. That's the beginning. Once your mind, body, or spirit sees how changing your moves can change your life, you're already halfway there.

2. *Stimulation.* The movements help you change, and the change helps you widen your perspective. Each change contains the seeds of another.

3. *Culmination*. You've done a lot of work, and it's given you a deeper understanding of what you need and who you are. At this point, movement practice becomes a bridge to real transformation; walk across it to a paradigm shift, and you've changed your life.

4. *Maintenance*. Life evolves, and growth continues. The movement practice will keep you on track through all the changes life inevitably brings. It will keep you from getting stale. Life, after all, is a process of never arriving. With consciousness and practice, the Moving Affirmations will keep you going in the direction that's right for you.

For me, the process is well summed up by the late singer-actress Portia Nelson in her "Autobiography in Five Short Chapters." Here it is:

Chapter 1
I walk down the street.
There is a deep hole in the sidewalk.
I fall in.
I am lost . . . I am helpless.
It isn't my fault.
It takes forever to find a way out.

Chapter 2
I walk down the same street.
There is a deep hole in the sidewalk.
I pretend I don't see it.
I fall in again.
I can't believe I am in this same place.
But, it isn't my fault.
It still takes a long time to get out.

Chapter 3
I walk down the same street.
There is a deep hole in the sidewalk.
I see it is there.
I still fall in . . . it's a habit . . . but,
my eyes are open.
I know where I am.
It is *my* fault.
I get out immediately.

Chapter 4
I walk down the same street.
There is a deep hole in the sidewalk.
I walk around it.

Chapter 5
I walk down another street.[7]

Nothing Is Forever

Not every change is permanent, and certainly not every change persists for every minute of the day. Sometimes we go back and visit those streets we thought we'd left behind. No one is centered 24/7, and no one is 100-percent free of those blockages that limit their lives. Old issues resurface, and new issues arise. Even people who have been committed to this movement practice for years, who have done the movements regularly, who are attuned to the need to address issues as they present themselves—even those people fall off center and lose focus. It's important to acknowledge this as a natural part of the process.

Despite all my years of Tai Ji practice, my wide experience in "reading" other people's bodies and my own, and a life that's fairly well centered and grounded, I still have places where I get hooked. From time to time, I find myself going off center—feeling frustrated or even fearful. At those moments, I assess the situation with something a friend calls "FID"—frequency, intensity, and duration. Invariably, my frustration—my off-center feeling—either occurs less often, is less difficult to get through, or doesn't last as long as the last one. This has proven true time after time over the years—not just for me, but also for all the students I've worked with. Yes, we fall. But we do so less often, with less intense impact, and for less time over the years. The conclusion seems obvious: The more we practice the movements, the less chance there is of becoming uncentered or ungrounded, and the easier it is to get back to center again. Bottom line? Personal growth through movement practice works.

So don't judge yourself—just get up and start again without wasting time on berating yourself. Life happens. If we're conscious and compassionate with ourselves and others, it makes it a little easier.

Contraction and Expansion

Breathe. Be aware of how your lungs expand as you inhale and contract when you exhale. Watch the waves on the shore—in, out, in, out—driven by the tides that ebb and flow. Think of how the moon waxes and wanes without fail, marking the months. This constant rise and fall is a basic law of nature. Expansion follows contraction; contraction follows expansion. It's the way life works, and it's all part of the process.

Yet many people have a tendency to judge the contraction phases of their lives. To them, contraction means that they're not moving, or they're not-growing, and they perceive it as a failure. Consequently, they simply withdraw. I've seen this happen with some of my students. Frustrated that they're "no longer progressing," they step back.

They stop doing what's good for them and they abandon their movement practice. It's as if they're saying to themselves: "If I can't *progress*, I may as well *regress*. If I can't go forward, I'll let myself go back."

I know what this feels like because I've been there. I've taken myself off the path of personal growth more than once—through frustration, disappointment, and confusion. Of course, I came back. I only wish someone had told me that contraction is part of the process, that it's a necessary part of expansion, and that taking a vacation from movement practice is a good thing. What *isn't* good is judging yourself. So take a break and enjoy it. You'll come back when you're ready.

Like the ocean, every move you make is governed by a tidal flow of breath. The very essence of life—the energy at your core—moves to a regular rhythm of contraction and expansion that's reflected in the way you move. As you begin to change your movements, take your time. Cherish the ebbing of growth as well as its flow. And if you can't quite cherish it, at least accept it as inevitable.

Find Your Own Pace

Change occurs at a rate corresponding to the frequency and focus of your practice. That's an obvious point, but it's one worth making. While I can't give you a guarantee of how fast your own growth will occur, I can promise you this: Transformation comes faster the more often you practice.

The process is more successful when you do the work assiduously, conscientiously, and with clear, maximum concentration. Doing the practice daily means giving yourself a regular reminder to modify a behavior. Every movement becomes a trigger that can spark change, or perhaps simply reaffirm a way of being.

Don't berate yourself if you don't practice every day; there's no benefit to self-flagellation. The changes you're undertaking can be profound, and only you know when you're ready for them. If you find that you're practicing less often than you think you should, it may be your body's way of telling you that this isn't the right time for you—and timing is important.

Practice isn't supposed to be hard labor, and it isn't punishment. It's focus, attention, and gentle movement, so that in time, you'll find yourself in harmony with your true essence and with the world around you.

To find your own pace, think of what the practice is doing for you. These movements are fertilizing the soil for change. As you grow comfortable doing them, you'll also grow more comfortable with yourself. You'll feel better about life, as you find that you're operating in the world in a more balanced way.

So don't be impatient, don't give up, and go at your own speed. The transformation will happen. You'll succeed in making the changes you want to make, and those changes will deepen over time. Notice when you're making progress, and appreciate yourself for the work you've done.

And as you walk down the path of your life, remember to enjoy the journey. Celebrate *every move you make.*

E
V
E
R
Y

M
O
V
E

Y
O
U

M
A
K
E

Endnotes

1. Pert, Candace B. *Molecules of Emotion: Why You Feel the Way You Feel.* Simon & Schuster, 1997.

2. Leonard, George. *The Way of Aikido: Life Lessons from an American Sensei.* Plume, 2000.

3. "The American Dance," published in *Modern Dance,* ed. by Virginia Stewart, 1935.

4. Williamson, Marianne. *A Return to Love: Reflections on the Principles of "A Course in Miracles."* HarperCollins, 1996.

5. Greene, Graham. *The Ministry of Fear,* Viking Press, 1993.

6. Paraphrased from *The Tao of Pooh,* by Benjamin Hoff. Viking Press, 1983.

7. Nelson, Portia. *There's A Hole In My Sidewalk: The Romance of Self-Discovery.* Beyond Words Publishing Co., 1994.

Appendix A

Suggested Affirmations

Try some of these affirmations to support your intentions as you do your movements, or let them inspire you to create your own positive messages. Remember: You should choose thoughts you can *accept*.

I am at peace.
I am centered and creative.
I trust the universe to guide me.
I am safe.
I accept myself as I am.
I listen to my inner voice.
I make wise choices.
I have good judgment.
I have love in my life.
I am lovable.
I value myself.
I am responsible for my life.
I am free.
I see the beauty in life.
I express freely and clearly who I am.
I meet life's challenges with strength.
I handle life with grace.
I flow with life.
I am fully alive.
I feel harmonious with the universe.
I have purpose in life.
I believe in myself.

E
V
E
R
Y

M
O
V
E

Y
O
U

M
A
K
E

I am loving.
I am open.
I am balanced.
I am serene.
I am content with myself.
I am content with my choices.
I have free choice.
I move forward in life.
I can release what I do not need.
I feel complete as I am.
My heart is open to love.
I am willing to share myself.
I show myself as I really am.
I love myself as I am.
I move in a relaxed way.
I will (do) enjoy each moment.
I am present with each moment.
I feel confident in myself. I am confident.
I deserve success.
I am open to abundance.
I have abundance.
I feel strong.
I accept love in my life.
I deserve love.
I trust the journey.
I am creative.
I can embrace my fears.
I can face my fears safely.
I surrender to my feelings or I am safe to surrender to my feelings.
I can create a positive path to follow.
I am open to support.
I am open to following my path, my passion, my heart.

I have courage.
I release my old unworkable patterns.
I deserve a supportive relationship.
I am unlimited. I feel boundless.
I release my disappointments.
I release my attachments.
I accept a healed state.
I trust a higher power to guide my journey.
I am open to solutions.
I create beauty in my life.
I accept my inner beauty.
I am supportive and supported.
Every moment unfolds with perfection.
I support myself and others.
I embrace my fears.
I embrace life's challenges with grace and strength.
I am beautiful.
I am loveable.
I am responsible for my life.
I am creating the life I want.
I have faith in the goodness of life.
I am filled with light.
I am filled with joy.
I am taking the necessary steps toward . . .
I now have choices.
I am strong.
I can take care of myself.
I can handle it.
I am okay just the way I am.
I am attractive.
I did the best I could.
I can choose what/who I want in my life.

Appendix B

Musical Selections to Accompany Your Moving Affirmations

Wolfgang Amadeus Mozart:
   Piano Concerto No. 21

Peter Kater & R. Carlos Nakai:
   Migration (Silver Wave, 1992)
   Natives (Silver Wave, 1990)
   Through Windows & Walls (Silver Wave, 2001)

David Darling:
   Eight Strings Religion (Wind Over the Earth, 2001)
   Cello Blue (Hearts of Space, 2001)

Peter Davison:
   Adagio: Music for T'ai Chi (The Orchard, 2000)

Michael Hoppe:
   Afterglow (Hearts of Space, 1999)

Kevin Kern:
   Embracing the Wind (Real Music, 2001)

Merlin's Magic:
   The Heart of Reiki (Inner World Records, 2000)

Appendix C

Photos of the
Moving Affirmations

continued on
next page

continued on
next page

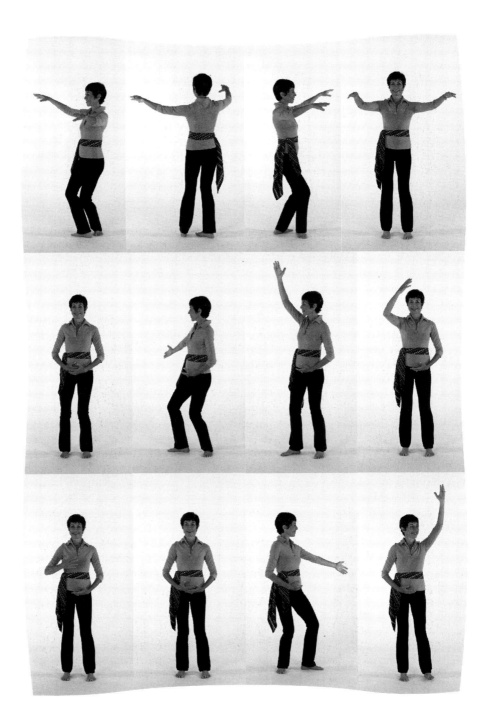

continued on
next page

Acknowledgments

So many people have contributed to my life, and thus, to my book. I'm glad to have the opportunity to acknowledge them here—and to express my gratitude.

I must first thank my mother, who never stopped me from moving and always encouraged me to dance without restrictions.

To all my students everywhere, who have opened themselves to learning and growing, and who have taught me so much in return, thank you.

Thanks also to all the Tai Ji, Qigong, and Shintaido teachers who have taught me so much for so many years. Special thanks to Al Chungliang Huang, who first inspired me to use movement, Tai Ji, and dance as a means for growth. The beautiful movements I learned from him are the basis of the Moving Affirmations in this book.

I'm grateful to a number of individuals whom I've always considered my mentors: Ram Dass and Stewart Emery taught me to step out of the box, expand my mind, and see life's possibilities from a broad perspective; John Gray and Harold Bloomfield encouraged me to believe in myself and taught me to trust my instincts in my work and my life; and Sally Nelson supported my growth in so many wonderful ways. Thanks to you all.

Robyn Bailis, one of the wondrous beings of this world, provided the constant friendship I so rely on. Sally Jessy Raphaël and Karl Soderland, clients and friends, provided their usual generosity of heart and spirit. They also introduced me to Harriet Norris, who tirelessly helped me with encouragement, ideas, support, time, suggestions, and friendship. Thanks to Sally Jessy and to Karl for that—and thanks, of course, to Harriet.

I'm grateful to Danny Levin of Hay House for taking a chance on a new author, and to Susanna Margolis, without whom I could not have become an author. You both do what you do brilliantly.

Annie Webster gave me the special opportunity to work with her and the "boys" (and girls). I thank her for it. Thank you, Joe Mello, for all your help in making this book a reality.

Thanks to Gloria Rosenstein for her invaluable suggestions.

I am grateful to Suzanne Spector, Jan Berlin, and Lisa Wenger for all their support; and to all my friends and clients in Del Mar for their encouragement and good wishes.

Most of all, I want to express my gratitude to Michael, my very loving husband, my best friend, and my favorite dance partner. He has been there in every way possible—with love, writing suggestions, and intellectual challenges. His willingness to grow and learn and stick with me through everything is a thing of beauty. He continues to be a model for the kind of person I want to be.

About the Author

Nikki Winston has been teaching movement therapy and Tai Ji since 1980. In 1988, she developed the first Tai Ji program at the renowned Golden Door fitness spa and directed it for ten years. There, she wrote and produced her award-winning Tai Ji video, *The Golden Door's Response to Stress*.

Today, Nikki maintains a private counseling practice, leads her own weeklong programs throughout the U.S. and Europe, and conducts workshops and training seminars for Fortune 500 companies, international conferences, medical schools, and foundations. Nikki's groundbreaking work has been featured in numerous publications, books, and on television.

Nikki completed her undergraduate work at the University of Geneva, Switzerland, and received her MBA from Columbia University in New York. She and her husband live in Del Mar, California.

You can contact Nikki by e-mailing her at: **nikki@nikkiwinston.com** or visit **www.nikkiwinston.com.**

We hope you enjoyed this Hay House book.
If you would like to receive a free catalog featuring additional
Hay House books and products, or if you would like information
about the Hay Foundation, please contact:

Hay House, Inc.
P.O. Box 5100
Carlsbad, CA 92018-5100

(760) 431-7695 or **(800) 654-5126**
(760) 431-6948 (fax) or **(800) 650-5115 (fax)**
www.hayhouse.com

Published and distributed in Australia by:
Hay House Australia, Ltd. • 18/36 Ralph St. • Alexandria NSW 2015 •
Phone: 612-9669-4299 • *Fax:* 612-9669-4144 • www.hayhouse.com.au

Published and distributed in the United Kingdom by:
Hay House UK, Ltd. • Unit 202, Canalot Studios • 222 Kensal Rd., London W10 5BN •
Phone: 44-20-8962-1230 • *Fax:* 44-20-8962-1239 • www.hayhouse.co.uk

Published and distributed in the Republic of South Africa by:
Hay House SA (Pty), Ltd., P.O. Box 990, Witkoppen 2068 •
Phone/Fax: 2711-7012233 • orders@psdprom.co.za

Distributed in Canada by:
Raincoast • 9050 Shaughnessy St., Vancouver, B.C. V6P 6E5 •
Phone: (604) 323-7100 • *Fax:* (604) 323-2600

Sign up via the Hay House USA Website to receive the Hay House online
newsletter and stay informed about what's going on with your favorite authors.
You'll receive bimonthly announcements about: Discounts and Offers,
Special Events, Product Highlights, Free Excerpts, Giveaways, and more!